"Pam is hands down one of the best cooks I know. She understands what works at home (and what doesn't) and writes clear, precise recipes that almost cook themselves. Pam's food perfectly balances effort with reward, proving that simplicity is the key to happiness in the kitchen."

—**JACK BISHOP**, chief creative officer, *America's Test Kitchen*

"Pam Anderson long ago cracked the code of quick weeknight cooking. Now she updates her wisdom with modern ingredients, tips, and techniques. As an overworked professional and food lover, I have just two words in response: Thank you."

—**JOE YONAN**, editor, *America the Great Cookbook*

HOW TO COOK
WITHOUT A BOOK

COMPLETELY UPDATED AND REVISED

How to Cook

—

Without a Book

—

**RECIPES AND TECHNIQUES
EVERY COOK SHOULD KNOW BY HEART**

PAM ANDERSON

PHOTOGRAPHS BY **LAUREN VOLO**

CLARKSON POTTER/PUBLISHERS
NEW YORK

Published in the United States by
Clarkson Potter/Publishers, an imprint of
the Crown Publishing Group, a division of
Penguin Random House LLC, New York.

crownpublishing.com
clarksonpotter.com

CLARKSON POTTER is a trademark
and POTTER with colophon is a
registered trademark of Penguin
Random House LLC.

Library of Congress Cataloging-in-
Publication Data has been applied for.

ISBN 978-1-5247-6166-0
Ebook ISBN 978-1-5247-6167-7

Printed in China

Book and cover design by Mia Johnson

Photographs by Lauren Volo

10 9 8 7 6 5 4 3 2 1

FIRST EDITION

to ALL COOKS
WHO GATHER PEOPLE
TO THE TABLE AS
OFTEN AS THEY CAN

Contents

Introduction

In the spring of 2000, I published *How to Cook Without a Book*. With my first book—*The Perfect Recipe*—launched, it was now time to share with other working parents how I finally overcame the challenge of getting dinner on the table. Eighteen years later and I am still receiving royalty checks. In 2013, *How to Cook Without a Book* made Buzzfeed's "19 Cookbooks That Will Improve Your Life" list. Says Ree Drummond, "It isn't glossy, fancy, or full of photographs, but it single-handedly altered the way I approach cooking by showing me how to take a small handful of cooking techniques and use them to create literally endless variations for breakfast, lunch, and dinner. I recommend it to anyone trying to find their footing in the kitchen!"

Over the years, many have suggested that I dust up and republish *How to Cook Without a Book*, but I always demurred because so much had changed, both in the food world and in me. My book was a teenager by now, and I knew better than to try to change a teen. What I could do, however, was to write again in that same spirit—a how-to that made sense for this time, one that taught people how to cook without reading a recipe.

THE BACKSTORY

How to Cook Without a Book was born of my struggles as a 1990s working mom trying to get dinner on the table. For months, I'd walk in the door at 6:30 p.m. to two hungry kids and a kitchen-clueless spouse. I'd frantically open the refrigerator door and stare. I saw ingredients, not dinner. The two big barriers to weeknight cooking were finding a recipe and grocery shopping. I knew how to get a recipe and shop for everything I needed to nail it—I was a magazine food editor, for God's sake—but when it came to feeding my family on a Wednesday night, this was a recipe for frustration.

Working in New York City, I was a long way from home, a world away from my Alabama mother and grandmother, who pulled off weeknight cooking without breaking a sweat. How did they do it? I wondered. True, my mother didn't work outside the home, though she had her hands full sewing, cleaning, caring for a child, running errands, volunteering, helping Dad fix up a handyman special, then building and maintaining her dream home. My grandmother was a dirt farmer, and later in life worked full-time in a garment factory making pajamas. Yet both of these women could do something I couldn't: regularly get dinner on the table.

I had access—literally—to thousands of ingredients they'd never heard of, and had made everything from crème caramel to cassoulet, but I was missing something. By keeping their pantry, fridge, and freezer stocked and relying on a set of internalized techniques and formulas, my mother and grandmother overcame both of the barriers to weeknight cooking: recipes and running to the store.

Following their example, I quit shopping ad hoc and stocked my kitchen. Eventually I developed my own set of techniques and formulas that worked for my busy life. In other words, I started to cook without a book. Regardless of the season, I could walk in the kitchen and start cooking with whatever ingredients I had around. With a few staples, I could transform chicken breasts, broccoli, lemons, and rice into a sautéed chicken breast dinner complete with a restaurant-style citrus pan sauce, a quick comforting soup, or a kick-ass stir-fry. With a carton of eggs, a seasonal vegetable, and a little cheese, I could whip up a supper frittata or a super-size omelet. And for years, I found a way to carry on like Mom and Mama Skipper, bringing my family around the table for dinner nearly every night.

THE CHANGING FOOD SCENE

Now that all seems like ages ago.

I still use many of the techniques and formulas I developed for *How to Cook Without a Book*, but in the last two decades, food and diet have shifted dramatically, and both my lifestyle and my cooking style have evolved.

I was proud in the nineties that hearts of romaine (not my mother's iceberg) dominated my salad bowl. Twenty years later, hardy dark greens like kale and beet tops are my new lettuces. And what used to be side dishes—butternut squash, Brussels sprouts, cauliflower, and carrots—I now roast, drizzle with vinaigrette, and call salad.

I still enjoy the occasional sautéed boneless, skinless chicken breast with a pan sauce, but meatier, more flavorful chicken thighs have gradually taken their place. You'll find fewer oversize Styrofoam trays of steaks and double Cryovac packages of pork tenderloin sitting in my Costco cart. I'm serving up more meatless meals and using meat as flavoring. And when I do choose meat, I no longer dirty three pans—one for meat, one for starch, and another for the vegetable. I mostly cook in one pot, one skillet, one large roasting pan, or on one oversize baking sheet.

A new book would need to account for the sea change in food preferences since *How to Cook Without a Book* came out at the turn of the century.

THE TIME CRUNCH—
NEW GENERATION, SAME PROBLEM

Like my grandmother in the thirties, my mother in the sixties, like me in the nineties, both of my daughters are married. They both work full time, as do their husbands. One is a mother. Watching their lives, I see the pattern repeating—except that my kids seem to have even less time than I did. They want to make healthy meals with ingredients they feel good about eating. And since they grew up with regular family dinners, they understand their importance and try to make them a priority. But like me at that stage of life, there are so many things competing with their need to eat well. I see not only the challenges of my generation, but also the particular stresses of the next generation.

The key, I've found, is not to think that eating well would mean you somehow had more time than anyone else. It's true, you have to take time for what matters; but the fact is, without a lot more time, you can still eat well. *How to Cook Without a Book: Recipes and Techniques Every Cook Should Know by Heart* is designed to reflect both the contemporary time crunch and the way my kids' generation, especially, thinks about food and the way we eat now.

A NEW MIND (NOT A NEW RECIPE)

At first I thought updating *How to Cook Without a Book: Recipes and Techniques Every Cook Should Know by Heart* meant simply freshening the ingredient list and making it quicker, but as I started to update the recipes and tweak the techniques, I soon stopped. The issue was bigger than that. You don't just need to know *how* to cook. You need to start thinking ahead and prepping like a cook.

Cooking dinner isn't about the twenty hellish minutes before you have to put something on the table—or face the pangs of your own hunger or the wrath of others. You stop for five minutes when you walk by a shop and see a basket of tomatoes and a ball of fresh mozzarella that would be perfect—not for tonight, but for Thursday night when you know you won't be home until late. As you cook tonight's dinner, you mindfully drop that ham hock in a pot of water so tomorrow's supper soup simmers to perfection in thirty minutes. You never boil just enough rice or pasta for tonight's dinner—you double it, so that tomorrow's fried rice, legume and grain salad, or lo mein is already under way.

What energizes this book is my own development as a cook. Part of it is simply being in the kitchen these last eighteen years, and the culinary breadth and depth that come with daily practice. I'm calmer, more confident. I'm a grandmother now, too, and I know that while cooking is still about getting it on the table, it's also about feeding, nurturing, and connecting with the people you love. So many years ago when I chose "cookdaily" as my e-mail address, I didn't fully understand its significance; but this way of life—cooking daily—is engrained in my being. It's no longer what I do—it's who I am. I don't imagine that someone can read one book and know what I know. What I can do is help people to think of what they eat, and how they make it, in a new way. Here's how it works.

SHOP LIKE A PRO

No matter how dramatically the food scene has changed, cooking at home with ease still starts with being well stocked. Whether you frequent one of the big-box stores, your local grocery store, the farmers' market, or some combination, you have to scout for good food and make sure you always have the basics on hand. I have an app for food shopping (AnyList), and my frequently used staples never come off the list. Ingredients like canned tomatoes, cartoned broth, and boxed pasta last for years in the pantry. A hunk of Parm, a jar of pesto in the fridge, a bag of shrimp or sausage in the freezer—any one of these ingredients could be the inspiration for a quick dish on a harried night. I call it money in the bank.

Seasonal fruits and vegetables are more fragile, so you can't overstock. Still, keep yourself supplied. As you pass through the produce department on your way to that quick gallon of milk or loaf of bread, grab a head of cauliflower, bunch of asparagus, or carton of cherry tomatoes. When you've got a few strategies for making dinner, you start to see how random ingredients like these are the building blocks of a great yet simple dinner.

DON'T STOP THINKING
ABOUT TOMORROW

A cook is always thinking ahead. As I get into the kitchen I naturally ask, "What am I cooking now that will help me pull off the next meal?" Occasionally, I'll double a pan of lasagna or pot of chili so I can freeze half for some night when I have zero time. But more often it's simpler, quicker ways to increase my stores. Why turn on the oven (or grill in the summer) to roast one pan of vegetables, when it takes only a few more minutes to make two? One for now and one tucked in the fridge. If you're caramelizing a skillet of onions for tonight's turkey burgers, it takes almost no time to double it. A container of roasted vegetables or caramelized onions means you can easily pull off really good pizza, full-flavored pasta, or an abundant frittata. If you're going to get out the blender or food processor and make vinaigrette for tonight's salad, it's just as easy to make a batch for the week. If there's a jar of homemade dressing in the fridge, it's much easier to get excited about salad as a main course.

NEW TECHNIQUES THAT TURN
GROCERIES INTO DINNER

With a decently stocked pantry, a little something in your culinary bank, and a few techniques and formulas committed to memory, you will eat very well. My shove-it-in-the-oven technique is just as it sounds. Toss all the ingredients in a roasting pan—there's an easy formula to follow—and slip it in the oven. Forty-five minutes later, catch a whiff of Chicken Tagine (page 258), Chili Chicken Stew with Black Beans and Corn (page 260), or Roast Italian Sausages with Potatoes and Cabbage (page 258). The added bonus is leftovers for tomorrow's lunch or dinner.

For even quicker oven meals, spice-rub a small cut of meat or fish and roast it, along with a couple of vegetables, on a couple of rimmed baking sheets. Whether it's spring salmon, asparagus, and new potatoes or cool-weather pork tenderloin, winter squash, and Brussels sprouts, this irresistibly fragrant petite roast dinner will emerge from the oven in twenty-five unattended minutes.

Weeknight tomato sauce is a few simple ingredients and a quick ten minutes. Why not open four cans instead of one? Once your pot of sauce is done, siphon off some for tonight's pasta with stir-ins like prosciutto, chickpeas, and a splash of cream; or canned tuna, capers, and pepper flakes. Add chicken, Indian spices, and a can of coconut milk to the second batch of sauce for quick Chicken Tikka Masala (page 123). Brown a couple of Italian sausages for the final batch of sauce and serve it over a mound of creamy polenta.

Plop another rotisserie chicken on the dinner table and the natives will groan. Instead, buy two chickens and quickly transform tonight's whole legs into Fig-Glazed Double-Roasted Chicken Legs (pages 223 to 224). Simmer the bones and use some of the meat for tomorrow's pot of Simple Posole (page 226) or Chicken-Corn Chowder (page 227). Shred the breast meat for barbecue chicken sandwiches, chicken salad, or tacos and quesadillas.

There are simple strategies for meatless meals as well. Legumes and grains make substantial year-round salads. Whether you serve chilled Lemony Lima Bean and Rice Salad with Asparagus and Fennel (page 110) in the spring or Lentil and Brown Rice Salad with Brussels Sprouts, Walnuts, and Cranberries (page 110) warm in the fall, the technique is the same year round.

THREE REASONS TO DO THIS

1. No one cares about what you and your family eat more than you do. Food cooked at home is better than most anything you'd pick up in the freezer case or drive-thru or what you'd eat at or take out of the average restaurant.

2. Cooking is a great way to keep families connected. At the dinner table for sure, but I've noticed when I start caramelizing onions, sizzling garlic, and simmering broth, the kitchen naturally draws hungry souls. As I glance up from my cutting board and inquire about the day, I usually find out what's really going on.

3. Finally, eating at home is cheaper than buying prepared foods and eating out. It's rare I don't look at a restaurant tab and do the math—how many great home-cooked meals and better bottles of wine I could have enjoyed with disposable income left over to do more lasting, interesting things. With one daughter and son-in-law saving for a down payment on a home, another daughter and son-in-law setting aside for their son's education, and David and I still working to finish building our retirement home, we all need to save.

EAT BETTER, FEEL BETTER

Health experts keep telling us that many of our persistent problems—childhood obesity, diabetes, autoimmune disorders, and high blood pressure, as well as anxiety and depression—come not only from *what* we eat but *how* we eat. It's not just that we need to eat better, more nutritious food; it's that almost two generations have forgotten how to cook. Science, in other words, is telling us what people have always known: Cooking good food and eating it together with loved ones and friends is the most basic human ritual. It is nourishment for the body and medicine for the spirit, with the power to bind people together in healthy families and communities.

It's easy to see that processed junk food can't do that. What we're now realizing is that even the best restaurants or take-out can't do that either. We have to go back into the kitchen, start dicing an onion, and watch as the magic of cooking begins to restore health and well-being in us and in those we love.

I said this eighteen years ago. Today, I believe it more than ever:
Give someone a recipe, they eat a meal.
Teach someone to cook, they eat for a lifetime.

How to Use This Book

Like the first edition, *How to Cook Without a Book* is simple to understand and easy to use. Chapters are divided into individual techniques and formulas. Taking them one at a time—divide-and-conquer style—makes them easy to master as each chapter works in unique ways.

Each chapter consists of five components:

- A step-by-step narrative of how the formula or technique works
- Photographs of the formula and technique's key steps
- A recipe presenting the formula or technique in its simplest form
- Simple variations exemplifying how the formula or technique works
- The key points of each formula or technique at a glance

In the step-by-step you learn the range and quantity of ingredients and an explanation of the technique or formula to ensure success. To enhance the narrative, there are also step-by-step photographs of the formula or technique's key steps.

For the novice cook, the formulas and techniques are written in recipe form, but after following it once or twice, you'll need only to review the at-a-glance points to make the dish.

To bring the formulas and techniques alive, there are variations following the recipe, but they are in no way exhaustive. After trying a few of them, you will be ready to spread your culinary wings and create your own variations.

A Full Larder

Most family schedules are erratic and unpredictable, and long-term meal planning can be frustrating, but running to the grocery store every day or two also takes time and energy most of us just don't have. Learning how to cook without a book starts with a well-stocked refrigerator, freezer, and pantry, because if you find yourself with an empty refrigerator at 6:00 p.m. on Wednesday night, you're more likely to go out or order in. Surrounding yourself with good food is the first step in effortless cooking.

When stocking your freezer, refrigerator, and pantry, you may get hit with sticker shock at the checkout, but when you think of what you would have spent if you had gone out for dinner even once, you quickly realize that food shopping is a bargain.

The following pantry, refrigerator, and freezer lists may look long. Many of the items are necessities (e.g., canned tomatoes, chicken broth, salt, onions, garlic, oil, vinegar), but others are not. Simply pick and choose from each list what looks good and makes sense for you. You probably have many of the ingredients in your kitchen now. And once you're stocked, it's just a matter of replenishing now and again. As time goes on, you will internalize the list and automatically know what's missing from week to week.

FRIDGE/FREEZER PROTEIN

Depending on your preferences, keep some of the following proteins in your refrigerator. And unless you plan to use it right away, freeze it. Make sure to wrap each cut of meat or seafood thoroughly and label it clearly. Slowly thaw it in the refrigerator the night before or thaw it quickly in the microwave, first on high power until it starts to thaw, then switching to defrost mode.

- Boneless, skinless chicken thighs and breasts and rotisserie chickens

- Fresh and cured/smoked sausages of any kind: pork, poultry, or lamb

- Beef steaks: boneless New York strip steaks, rib eyes, filet mignons

- Ground meat: beef, lamb, turkey, meatloaf mix

- Pork tenderloin

- Bacon

- Prosciutto

- A small hunk of ham or a spiral-cut ham: Both cuts last longer than sliced deli ham, and you can cut it the way you want—slices for sandwiches, julienne for salads, small dice for omelets, and large dice for soup. You can also roast it whole (see "Weeknight Roast Dinner," page 238). If you can't use what you've bought within a week, freeze some of it.

- Lamb chops or rack of lamb

- Fish fillets: salmon, thick flounder, catfish, snapper, tilapia, grouper

- Fish steaks: tuna or swordfish

- Extra-firm tofu and/or tempeh

- Frozen untreated (dry) sea and bay scallops

- Frozen large shrimp (preferably pink and wild)

OTHER GOODIES FOR THE FREEZER

- Frozen vegetables: green peas, greens, pearl onions, corn, artichoke hearts

- Good bread. If you don't have time to make Daily Bread (page 71), keep a couple of European-style crusty loaves in the freezer. It'll take any meal up a notch.

- Pizza crusts: If you don't have time to make Grilled Pizza Crusts (page 151) or Oven-Baked Pizza Crusts (page 152), keep a couple of store-bought crusts on hand.

- Yeast: If you bake bread or pizza crusts regularly, buy yeast in bulk and store it in the freezer, where it will keep longer.

- Orange juice concentrate, for the pan sauces.

REFRIGERATOR VEGETABLE AND FRUIT STAPLES

Buy good-looking fresh seasonal vegetables and fruits of your choice, like fennel and asparagus in the spring, green beans in the summer, Brussels sprouts in the fall, and winter squash and hardy greens in the winter.

Storage: For asparagus, snap off the tough ends and store them like flowers, stem ends in water, in the fridge. Extend the life of other vegetables, such as green beans and Brussels sprouts, by refrigerating them in zipper-lock freezer bags, pressing all of the air out of the bag. Store hardier vegetables, such as winter squash, potatoes, and onions, at cool room temperature.

In addition to seasonal fruits and vegetables, keep on hand the following:

- Carrots
- Celery
- Fresh herbs, such as cilantro, parsley, basil, and rosemary. Store them like asparagus (see Storage above), with a plastic bag covering the leaves, or like green beans in a zipper-lock bag with all the air removed before sealing. I also really like the tubed herbs in the refrigerated produce section of most well-stocked grocery stores.
- Dark salad greens, such as arugula, baby spinach, and kale
- Bell peppers
- Cabbage
- Scallions
- Citrus, such as lemons, limes, and oranges (Unless you go through them quickly, store them in the refrigerator.)
- Peeled garlic and refrigerated garlic paste
- Fresh ginger or refrigerated ginger paste

Although the following vegetables are not stored in the refrigerator, they are included in this section for ease. For extended life, keep them in a cool, dark place.

- Yellow, red, and/or sweet potatoes
- A bag of sweet or yellow onions
- Shallots
- Red onions

REFRIGERATOR DAIRY

Keep the following dairy items in the refrigerator:

- Milk

- Eggs

- Butter: Store it in the freezer if you don't use it often.

- Heavy cream: It has a relatively long shelf life and is great to have around for simple pan sauces.

- 3 to 4 cheeses of your choice: For me, that's good sharp Cheddar, blue or goat cheese, a chunk of Parmigiano-Reggiano, mozzarella for pizza, and feta.

- Greek yogurt, ricotta

PANTRY AND FRIDGE STAPLES

CANS, CARTONS, BOTTLES, AND JARS

- Olive oil

- Vegetable oil

- Sesame oil

- Vinegar: red wine, rice, balsamic, sherry

- Dijon mustard

- Mayonnaise

- Barbecue sauce

- Ketchup

- Bottled horseradish

- Roasted peppers

- Pesto

- Salsas: regular and verde

- Soy sauce: regular and dark (or molasses mixed with soy as a substitute for dark)

- Hoisin sauce

- Asian fish sauce

- Capers
- Chutney
- Red curry paste
- Olives: Kalamata and pimiento-stuffed
- Cornichons
- Cartons of chicken broth
- Bottled clam juice or fish broth
- Canned crushed tomatoes (or whole tomatoes packed in puree)
- Canned diced tomatoes
- Tomato paste, canned or in a tube
- Canned coconut milk, regular and light
- Canned beans (white, black, pinto, chickpeas) and hominy
- Canned whole baby clams
- Canned tuna
- Anchovies
- Evaporated milk

DRIED GRAINS, BEANS, AND LEGUMES

- Dried beans: white, black, pinto, chickpeas
- Dried pasta: spaghetti, egg noodles, small pasta such as ditalini, bite-size pasta such as ziti
- Lo mein and pad Thai noodles
- Couscous
- Rice: brown and white, such as basmati and jasmine
- Lentils and/or split peas
- Barley
- Quinoa
- Panko or plain dried breadcrumbs

FRUIT, SEEDS, NUTS, AND SWEETS

- Dried fruit: cranberries, cherries, apricots, prunes, figs, raisins, and/or currants
- Nuts: walnuts, almonds, pecans, peanuts, pine nuts, pistachios
- Seeds: hulled pumpkin seeds (pepitas), sunflower seeds
- Bittersweet or semisweet chocolate, to flavor chili
- Marmalade and jams
- Maple syrup and/or honey

BAKING AND SPICES

- Flour: unbleached all-purpose or bread
- Cornmeal
- Cornstarch
- Sugar: white and brown
- Salt and black peppercorns with a grinder
- Dried herbs: thyme, tarragon, oregano, basil
- Herb blends: herbes de Provence, Italian seasoning
- Garlic powder
- Paprika: smoked and sweet
- Ground spices: coriander, cumin
- Warm spices, such as ground cinnamon, nutmeg, cloves, and ginger
- Spice blends: chili powder, curry powder, garam masala
- Hot spices: red pepper flakes and cayenne pepper
- Whole spices: fennel and caraway seeds
- Bay leaves

WINE AND SPIRITS

- Red and white wine
- Fortified wines, such as dry vermouth, sweet sherry, Marsala wine, port

A Little Mise

Preparing a little extra at one meal—say, rice or simple
tomato sauce—or making something that takes
no effort when you've got time (like simmering a ham hock
or soaking a bag of lentils) makes it easy to say yes to
cooking on a night when you don't think you have
it in you. A container of vinaigrette or a tub of caramelized
onions sitting in the fridge gets you past that first hurdle—
figuring out what to make!

A Jar of Good Vinaigrette

You can always toss salad with olive oil and vinegar, but it's nice to have homemade vinaigrette—especially for tossing salads made with sturdy greens like kale or for drizzling over single or paired vegetable salads like a plate of asparagus, hot off the grill, or a mound of warm, roasted root vegetables.

All-Purpose Vinaigrette and Balsamic Vinaigrette are the two dressings I use the most. The all-purpose vinaigrette formula works for lemon juice as well as most any vinegar, including red wine, white wine, and sherry vinegars. The addition of mild, sweet rice vinegar rounds out the more acidic ingredients, while the hefty scoop of Dijon mustard ensures an appealing, emulsified dressing.

ALL-PURPOSE VINAIGRETTE

Makes about 1½ cups

2 large garlic cloves or 1 large shallot, minced

¼ cup fresh lemon juice, fresh lime juice, or vinegar (red wine, white wine, or sherry)

¼ cup Dijon mustard

2 tablespoons rice vinegar

Salt and ground black pepper

1 cup extra-virgin olive oil

1. Whisk the garlic, lemon juice or vinegar, mustard, rice vinegar, a big pinch of salt, and several grinds of pepper in a medium bowl or a 1-quart liquid measuring cup.

2. Slowly whisk in the oil (I frequently pull out my hand mixer fitted with the whisk attachment), first in droplets, then in a steady stream to make a thick vinaigrette. Pour into a jar and refrigerate. (Can be refrigerated for up to 1 month.)

BALSAMIC VINAIGRETTE

Makes scant 2 cups

2 large garlic cloves or 1 large shallot, minced

⅔ cup balsamic vinegar

¼ cup Dijon mustard

Salt and ground black pepper

1 cup extra-virgin olive oil

1. Whisk the garlic, vinegar, mustard, a big pinch of salt, and several grinds of pepper in a medium bowl or a 1-quart liquid measuring cup.

2. Slowly whisk in the oil (I frequently pull out my hand mixer fitted with the whisk attachment), first in droplets, then in a steady stream to make thick vinaigrette. Pour into a jar and refrigerate. (Can be refrigerated for up to 1 month.)

A Pan of Vegetables—
Roasted, Grilled, or Steam-Sautéed

If you've got cooked vegetables, you've got a good start on dinner. Whether they're grilled, roasted, or steam-sautéed, drizzle the vegetables with vinaigrette and serve them warm, room temperature, or chilled as a salad. Or use the cooked vegetables to make a quick soup, pasta, or frittata, or as an instant topping for pizza.

ROASTED VEGETABLES

Why only roast one pan of vegetables for tonight's dinner when it only takes a couple of extra minutes of prep and a smidgen of oven energy to roast a second one at the same time? Enjoy the first pan of roasted vegetables tonight and use the second pan to jump-start dinner another night. If roasting two pans, adjust the second oven rack to the upper-middle position. At the 20-minute mark, switch pans, giving them a quick stir, and also rotate them back to front. Continue to roast until the vegetables are golden, 10 to 15 minutes longer.

To measure the vegetables quickly, pull out a 2-quart liquid measuring cup and fill it to the brim for each pan. Or simply fill two 18 x 12-inch rimmed baking sheets with vegetables, making sure they fit snugly in a single layer.

COMMON ROASTING VEGETABLES

- **Carrots, sweet potatoes, parsnips, rutabagas, and turnips:** Peel and cut into large chunks.
- **Red, yellow, or white onions:** Peel and cut into large chunks.
- **Golden beets:** Peel, halve if small, quarter if medium, and cut into large chunks if big.
- **Winter squash:** Peel, seed, and cut into large chunks (or buy already peeled and cut winter squash).
- **Asparagus:** Snap off tough ends.
- **Potatoes (any kind):** Halve if small, quarter if medium, and cut into large chunks if big.
- **Leeks:** Trim dark green part, halve lengthwise, wash to remove potential grit, and cut crosswise into 1½-inch sections.
- **Shallots:** Peel, leave whole if medium, halve if large.
- **Frozen pearl onions:** Leave frozen.

- **Fennel:** Trim, core, and cut into large chunks.
- **Zucchini and yellow squash:** Trim, halve lengthwise—quarter if large—and cut into large chunks.
- **Eggplant (any kind):** Trim and cut into large chunks.
- **Bell peppers (any color):** Halve, stem, seed, and cut into thick strips.
- **Cauliflower:** Core, break into florets, halve large florets.
- **Cherry tomatoes:** Leave whole.
- **Mushrooms (cremini or domestic white):** Halve if large, leave whole if medium or small.

A PAN OF ROASTED VEGETABLES

Makes about 6 cups (serves 6 to 8)

You can toss the vegetables with herbs (dried or fresh woody) *before* roasting or with fresh herbs after (see Note).

A heaping 8 cups vegetables (see "Common Roasting Vegetables," page 36–37)

3 tablespoons olive oil

Dried or fresh herbs (optional; see Note)

Salt and ground black pepper

---

1. Adjust the oven rack to the lowest position and heat the oven to 450°F. Coat a large (18 × 12-inch) rimmed baking sheet with vegetable cooking spray.

2. Toss the vegetables of choice with the oil, dried herb (if using), and a generous sprinkling of salt and pepper. With the exception of asparagus, turn the vegetables onto the baking sheet and roast for 20 minutes.

3. Remove the vegetables from the oven and stir (add asparagus, if using, at this point). Return to the oven and continue roasting until cut sides are lightly brown, about 10 minutes longer. Remove from the oven and toss with fresh herb (if using); serve.

Note: *Before* roasting, toss vegetables with 1 teaspoon dried herbs (such as thyme, tarragon, basil, oregano, herbes de Provence, or Italian seasoning) or 1 tablespoon chopped fresh woody herbs (such as rosemary or thyme leaves). Or *after* roasting, toss vegetables with ¼ cup chopped fresh herbs (such as parsley, basil, or cilantro, or a couple of tablespoons of more assertive herbs like dill, sage, or tarragon).

At a Glance
ROASTED VEGETABLES

1. Toss the vegetables with oil, salt, and pepper.

2. Roast them on a rimmed baking sheet in a 450°F oven for 20 minutes.

3. Remove from the oven and stir.

4. Roast 10 minutes more.

THE EXCEPTIONS

Roasted red beets

Because red beets stain everything they touch, don't mix them with other vegetables. Instead, wash them, cut off any long stems down to the root, wrap each one in foil, and roast them on a baking sheet in a 400°F oven until a knife blade inserted in the largest one goes in easily, 30 minutes for small ones, 45 minutes for medium beets, and a full hour for large ones. (Use a toaster oven to save energy!) When they are cool enough to handle, peel (the skin slips off with your fingers) and cut into desired pieces.

Roasted Brussels sprouts

When roasted with a pan full of other vegetables, Brussels sprouts get done sooner and their cut surfaces don't brown. Put them in a pan by themselves and you can roast them to perfection. For 1 to 1½ pounds, halve the Brussels sprouts lengthwise and toss with olive oil, salt, and pepper, and place them cut side down on a rimmed baking sheet. Roast on the lowest oven rack at the same temperature as other vegetables (450°F) until tender and the cut sides are impressively browned, about 15 minutes.

For less than a pound of Brussels sprouts, pan-roast them on the stovetop in a 12-inch skillet using the steam-sauté method (see page 48). Place the Brussels sprouts in the pan, cut side down, and cook them until they are tender, all the liquid has evaporated, and the cut sides are impressively browned, 7 to 9 minutes. If you don't mind setting a roasting pan over two burners, you can double the space and steam-sauté up to 1½ pounds of Brussels sprouts on the stovetop, saving time.

GRILLED VEGETABLES

If you've got a grill, it's even quicker and easier to score extra vegetables for your larder, and the same reasoning for roasting extra applies to the grill. Why fill only half the rack when, with a few more minutes of prep, you could grill an entire rack of vegetables? Cooking on a grill rack means small vegetables like mushrooms can slip through, so avoid them and make sure to cut vegetables for grilling a little larger than those for roasting. You can always cut them into smaller pieces once they come off the grill.

COMMON GRILLING VEGETABLES

- **Medium carrots and parsnips:** Peel and halve lengthwise. If they're very long (10 to 12 inches), you may want to halve them crosswise.
- **Medium sweet potatoes:** Peel and slice lengthwise into slabs ½ to ¾ inch thick.
- **Small onions:** Do not peel; halve lengthwise or crosswise.
- **Large shallots:** Do not peel; halve lengthwise.
- **Turnips and rutabagas:** Peel and cut into slabs ½ to ¾ inch thick (halve lengthwise if large).
- **Medium golden beets:** Peel and cut into slabs ½ to ¾ inch thick (or halve small beets lengthwise).
- **Winter squash:** Peel, seed, and cut into slabs ½ to ¾ inch thick.
- **Asparagus:** Snap off tough ends.
- **New potatoes:** Halve. Cut bigger potatoes into slabs ½ to ¾ inch thick.
- **Small leeks:** Trim dark green part, halve lengthwise, and wash to remove grit.
- **Fennel:** Trim fronds, quarter small bulbs; cut larger ones into 6 to 8 wedges.
- **Bell peppers (any color):** Stem, quarter, and seed.
- **Small zucchini, eggplant, or yellow squash:** Halve lengthwise (if large, slice lengthwise into 3 or 4 pieces).
- **Small portobello mushrooms:** Stem.
- **Cauliflower:** Cut large florets into slabs.
- **Cabbage:** Cut into medium wedges, leaving core intact.

TIPS AND TRICKS

- Asparagus—especially pencil-thin asparagus—cooks more quickly than other vegetables, so grill them separately. Lay them across the grill rack so they don't fall through.

A GRILL FULL OF VEGETABLES

Makes about 6 cups (serves 8)

You can toss the vegetables with herbs (dried or fresh woody) *before* grilling or with fresh herbs after (see Note).

A generous 8 cups vegetables (see "Common Grilling Vegetables," page 42)

3 tablespoons olive oil

Salt and ground black pepper

Dried or fresh herbs (optional; see Note)

---

1. Heat a gas grill, igniting all burners on high for at least 10 minutes.

2. Meanwhile, toss the vegetables with oil and salt and pepper to taste, and dried herb (if using). Clean the hot grate with a wire brush, then lubricate it with an oil-soaked rag.

3. Arrange the prepared vegetables on the hot grill grate, being careful not to overcrowd (with the exception of asparagus spears, which are added when turning the vegetables at the halfway point).

4. Cover and cook the vegetables, turning them only once about halfway through, until they form impressive grill marks on both sides and are tender-crisp, about 10 minutes. Remove from the grill and toss with fresh herbs (if using).

Note: *Before* grilling, toss vegetables with 1 teaspoon dried herbs (such as thyme, tarragon, basil, oregano, herbes de Provence, or Italian seasoning) or 1 tablespoon chopped fresh woody herbs (such as rosemary or thyme leaves). Or *after* grilling, toss vegetables with a ¼ cup chopped fresh herbs (such as parsley, basil, or cilantro, or a couple of tablespoons of more assertive herbs like dill, sage, or tarragon).

At a Glance
GRILLED VEGETABLES

1. Heat the grill.

2. Toss the vegetables with oil, salt, and pepper to taste.

3. Arrange the vegetables on the hot grill grate.

4. Cover and cook the vegetables, turning once halfway through, until they form impressive grill marks on both sides and are tender-crisp, about 10 minutes.

STEAM-SAUTÉED VEGETABLES

When you need vegetables fast, use what I call the "steam/sauté" method. Exactly as it sounds, the vegetable is steamed, or "wet cooked," and then sautéed, or "dry cooked." This dual technique is seamlessly accomplished in the same pan. No steamer contraptions, no large quantities of water to boil, no awkward vegetable draining or cooling between steps. And no flavor loss!

COMMON STEAM-SAUTÉ VEGETABLES

- **Asparagus:** Snap off the tough ends.
- **Broccoli crowns:** Cut into florets (if using whole broccoli, peel stems and cut into ½-inch coins).
- **Broccolini:** No prep.
- **Brussels sprouts:** Trim and halve lengthwise.
- **Cabbage:** Quarter, core, and cut into thick shreds.
- **Carrots and parsnips:** Peel and slice into ½-inch-thick coins.
- **Cauliflower:** Remove core and cut into florets.
- **Green beans, snow peas, and sugar snap peas:** Trim.
- **Winter squash, turnips, and rutabagas:** Peel and cut into medium dice.

ADD-INS

When steam-sautéing vegetables, you really only need water for steaming, fat for sautéing, and salt for flavor, but you can add one or more of the following optional flavorings.

Add one or more of these at the beginning when you add the vegetables:

½ small onion, thinly sliced

2 garlic cloves, minced

1 tablespoon grated ginger root

1½ teaspoons chopped fresh woody herbs (thyme or rosemary)

¼ cup chopped olives: Kalamata or pimiento-stuffed green

2 tablespoons drained capers

2 tablespoons mustard: grainy, Dijon, or honey

1 tablespoon soy sauce

1 tablespoon lemon juice

½ teaspoon dried herbs: tarragon, thyme, oregano, Italian seasoning, or herbes de Provence

½ teaspoon caraway seeds

¼ teaspoon red pepper flakes

1 teaspoon curry powder or garam masala

½ teaspoon ground spices: cumin, ginger

¼ teaspoon ground or finely grated nutmeg

Add these after the vegetables have steamed and are starting to sauté:

2 tablespoons toasted seeds or chopped nuts: walnuts, pecans, hazelnuts, almonds, whole pine nuts, sunflower seeds, or pumpkin seeds

1 tablespoon chopped fresh soft herbs: basil, parsley, mint, chives, dill, tarragon, oregano, or cilantro

½ teaspoon finely grated citrus zests: lemon or orange

STEAM-SAUTÉED VEGETABLES

Makes about 4 cups

If the vegetable isn't cooked to your liking by the time the water has evaporated, simply add a couple more tablespoons of water, cover, and continue to cook until tender.

⅓ cup water

1 tablespoon olive oil, butter, or bacon drippings

½ teaspoon table salt

1 pound prepared vegetables (see "Common Steam-Sauté Vegetables," page 47)

Add-ins (optional; page 47)

Ground black pepper

---

1. Combine the water, oil, salt, vegetables, and any of the Add-ins that go in at this stage in a Dutch oven or a large, deep skillet. Cover, bring to a boil, and steam over medium-high heat until the vegetable is brightly colored and just tender, about 5 minutes, depending on the vegetable size.

2. Uncover and continue to cook until the liquid evaporates, 1 to 2 minutes longer (adding any of the Add-ins that go in at this stage). Sauté to intensify the flavors, 1 to 2 minutes longer. Adjust the seasonings, including pepper to taste, and serve.

At a Glance
STEAM-SAUTÉED VEGETABLES

1. Bring the water, fat, salt, and vegetables to a boil in a 12-inch covered skillet.

2. Steam over medium-high heat until the vegetables are just tender.

3. Uncover and continue to cook until the liquid evaporates.

4. Sauté to intensify the flavors.

Caramelized Onions, aka Culinary Gold

If there's one thing I make time for, it's caramelizing onions for the week. It's just so nice to reach into the fridge and pull out a container of caramelized onions to flavor scrambled eggs or a simple tomato sauce, top pizzas or cheese toast, or make a little tray of impromptu hors d'oeuvres.

Because it takes a lot of onions to get a decent-size container full, I start with 4 big sweet onions and cook them in a heavy-duty roasting pan set over two burners. The larger surface area means they cook down more quickly. If you don't have a roasting pan, simply caramelize the onions in two 12-inch skillets.

A ROASTING PAN OF CARAMELIZED ONIONS

Makes a scant quart

6 tablespoons olive oil

4 large sweet onions, halved and thinly sliced

1. Heat the oil over low heat in a large roasting pan set over 2 burners while you slice the onions. A few minutes before adding the onions, increase the heat to medium-high. Add the onions and cook, stirring often, until they are dramatically reduced and light caramel brown, about 10 minutes.

2. Reduce the heat to medium-low and continue to cook the onions, stirring frequently, until they are rich caramel in color, 20 to 30 minutes longer. (Can be cooled to room temperature, then refrigerated in a covered container for several weeks.)

Pickled Pink Onions

My son-in-law doesn't like raw onions, so he pickles them instead. When I saw how quick and easy it was, I started pickling them, too. Not only do pickled pink onions beautify any dish, but they taste better, too. And they save time! When serving salad or tacos for dinner or sandwiches for lunch, it means I don't have to start from scratch peeling and slicing raw onion. It's rare I don't have a tub of pickled *and* caramelized onions in my fridge— they make just about any dish more special or halve the recipe.

PICKLED PINK ONIONS

Makes 5 to 6 cups

2 large red onions, halved and thinly sliced

6 cups boiling water

1½ cups distilled white or rice vinegar

2 teaspoons kosher salt

Place the onions in a heatproof medium bowl and pour the boiling water over them. Let stand 15 seconds and then drain. Return to the bowl, pour the vinegar over them, and season with the salt. (You can use the pickled onions right away. The remainder can be refrigerated in a lidded tub or jar for a month or more.)

A Bowl of Greens—
Massaged Kale

Few of us have enough refrigerator space to hold a puffy balloon-size bag of washed and stemmed kale from the grocery story, but if you take a little time when you get home to remove the stray stems, tear the kale into bite-size pieces, and then massage it with a little oil, you will accomplish three things: You will dramatically reduce the bulk (and therefore increase refrigerator space), increase the life of the greens, and have prepared greens ready for salads, soups, frittatas, and pasta.

To massage kale and other hardy greens like collards and mustard greens, drizzle 2 tablespoons olive oil over 1 pound trimmed greens. Vigorously rub the greens in your fingertips until they have softened and been reduced in volume. Stuff the greens in a gallon-size zipper-lock bag, press all the air from the bag, seal it, and refrigerate. Stored this way, the greens will stay fresh a week or more.

A Few Boiled Eggs

Boiled eggs can jump-start just about any meal, so always keep a few on hand to toss into salads, to serve as meatless protein atop a hearty bean and grain salad, or to enjoy for breakfast. The same method works for larger quantities of eggs—just increase the surface area, making sure the eggs fit the pan in a single layer.

Cover 6 eggs with water in a medium saucepan. Cover the pan and bring to a full boil over medium-high heat. Remove from the heat and let the eggs stand, covered, for 10 minutes. Drain and run them under cold running water until the saucepan is decidedly cold; toss in a handful of ice and let stand in the water until cool. Boiled eggs in their shells can be refrigerated for up to 2 weeks.

A Bag of Beans or Legumes
(or a Couple of Cans Will Do)

Keep both bags and cans of beans on hand, because sometimes you'll have time to cook beans from scratch, and other times you'll just need to grab a couple of cans and start cooking. When cooking dried beans, there are ways to speed up the soaking and cooking process, but I prefer the slow (but effortless) soak method. If I'm in a hurry, I just open a can.

Canned lentils and split peas are not common, but they cook so quickly that you don't need the canned option. You don't have to soak lentils or split peas, but my unique method saves enough time that you can actually cook them from scratch—lentils in just 10 minutes, split peas in just 5!—for weeknight dinner. Unheard of!

COOKED LENTILS

Makes 5 to 6 cups

Canned lentils are hard to find and are not especially good, but the good news is that if you soak dried lentils, they cook in about 10 minutes, and in about 20 minutes if you don't, making it easy to cook up a batch to use throughout the week. Save your red and yellow lentils—which cook quickly and don't hold their shape as well as the brown, green, and black varieties—for dals and soups.

If you forget to soak the lentils, simply bring 5 cups water and 1 pound lentils to a boil in a covered 12-inch skillet. Reduce the heat to medium-low, cover, and cook until the water is almost absorbed and the lentils are just tender, 15 to 20 minutes. Let stand for a few minutes before using.

1 pound (2⅓ cups) black, brown, or green lentils or lentils du Puy

Table salt

1. Soak the lentils in 6 cups water and 1 tablespoon salt for at least 4 and up to 24 hours.

2. Drain the lentils and transfer to a 12-inch skillet. Add 3 cups water and ½ teaspoon salt. Cover and bring to a boil over medium-high heat, stirring once or twice, and skimming any foam. Reduce the heat to medium-low and cook until they are just tender, about 10 minutes. (Can be covered and refrigerated for several days or frozen for several months.)

COOKED BEANS

Makes a generous 6 cups

---

1 pound (2⅓ cups) dried beans, such as navy, Great Northern, pinto, kidney, black, or garbanzo

Table salt

---

1. Soak the beans at room temperature in 6 cups cold water and 1 tablespoon salt for at least 4 and up to 24 hours.

2. Drain the beans and transfer to a medium pot. Add 6 cups water and 1 teaspoon salt. Bring the beans to a boil over medium-high heat, reduce the heat to low, and cook, partially covered, skimming any foam, until the beans are tender, about 30 minutes. (Can be covered and refrigerated in their cooking liquid for several days or frozen for several months.)

A Word About Salt

In almost every case throughout this book, you should feel free to use whatever type of salt (kosher salt, table salt, fine sea salt, etc.) you have on hand. The only time I specify a type of salt is in the cooking water for boiling pasta, grains, legumes, etc. This is because a particular amount is needed and one tablespoon of table salt is saltier than one tablespoon of kosher salt. In these cases, if you only have kosher salt or coarse sea salt in your pantry, simply make sure that the cooking water is plenty salty.

COOKED SPLIT PEAS

Makes about 5 cups

Soaking and quickly cooking split peas means they hold their shape and don't get mushy, making them especially good in legume and grain salads. You can also turn them into soups. Since they're already cooked, it takes no time for them to break down and soften.

---

1 pound (2⅓ cups) green or yellow split peas

Table salt

---

1. Soak the split peas in 6 cups water and 1 tablespoon salt for at least 4 and up to 24 hours.

2. Drain the peas and transfer to a 12-inch skillet. Add 3 cups water and ½ teaspoon salt. Cover and bring to a boil over medium-high heat, stirring once or twice, and skimming any foam. Reduce the heat to low, cover, and cook until they are slightly soft but they still hold their shape, about 5 minutes. Drain and spread out on a rimmed baking sheet to cool before using. (Can be covered and refrigerated for several days or frozen for several months.)

A Cup of Grains
(That Would Be Pasta, Too!)

Whether it's cooked rice, barley, pasta, or quinoa, having a container of cooked grains in the fridge makes it easy to assemble a bean and grain salad, pull together a quick soup, or fire up the skillet for fried rice or lo mein.

Like split peas and lentils, you can dramatically reduce the time for long-cooking grains like barley and brown rice by soaking them. If you can simply remember to dump a couple of heaping cups of brown rice or barley into 6 cups water the night before or the morning of (or just 4 hours ahead), you can cook barley in 10 minutes and brown rice in 20. Cooking the grains in a large skillet and small amount of water means the water comes to a boil more quickly, which also reduces cooking time.

COOKED PASTA

Most of the pasta formulas in this book call for 12 ounces of pasta serving 4 people. While you're at it, cook a full pound, and you'll have 4 ounces of leftover cooked pasta that could be the start of a hearty bean and grain salad or just the right ingredient to bulk up that main course green salad or dinner soup. Note that I boil pasta in a smaller quantity of water and a larger amount of salt than most recipes call for, resulting in flavorful pasta that cooks quickly. (It takes a long time to bring a gallon of water to a boil!) Just so you know how much water to boil, measure it in a 2-quart liquid measuring cup.

Table salt

1 pound pasta, any shape

1. Bring a generous 2 quarts water and 1 tablespoon salt to a boil in a large soup kettle.

2. Add the pasta and, using the back-of-the-box times as a guide, cook, partially covered and stirring frequently at first to prevent sticking, until just tender. Drain, and if not using in a recipe, turn onto a rimmed baking sheet to cool. (Can be stored in a covered container for several days.)

PASTA PRESTO!

Like any other grain, pasta (yes, pasta!) can be soaked while you're sleeping or at work; and when you're ready, it cooks in about the same amount of time as fresh pasta—just a couple of minutes. Its texture is a little softer than unsoaked pasta, but the time saving is big.

8 ounces pasta (half a 1-pound box), any shape
Table salt

1. Soak the pasta at room temperature in 6 cups water and 1 tablespoon salt for at least 4 and up to 24 hours.

2. Bring 6 cups water and 1 teaspoon salt to a boil in a large pot. Drain the pasta, add it to the boiling water, and cook until just tender, a couple of minutes. (Angel hair cooks within seconds!) Drain and serve.

COOKED BARLEY

Makes about 6 cups

If you don't have time to soak the barley, simply bring 6 cups water and 1½ teaspoons salt to a boil over medium-high heat in a large saucepan. Add 1½ cups barley, cover, and reduce the heat to medium-low and simmer, partially covered until just tender, about 40 minutes

1 pound (2⅓ cups) pearled barley
Table salt

1. Soak the barley at room temperature in 6 cups water and 1 tablespoon salt for at least 4 and up to 24 hours.

2. Drain the barley and transfer to a 12-inch skillet. Add 3 cups water and ½ teaspoon salt. Cover and bring to a boil over medium-high heat. Reduce the heat to medium-low and simmer until tender, about 10 minutes. (Can be covered and refrigerated for several days or frozen for several months.)

COOKED QUINOA

Makes 7 cups

For added flavor, toast the quinoa first in a 12-inch skillet. Turn the burner to medium-high, stirring occasionally. When the quinoa starts to pop, stir constantly until it smells nutty and looks golden, 2 to 3 minutes longer.

1 pound (2½ cups) quinoa (red, white, or a mix)
Table salt

Bring the quinoa, 4½ cups water, and 1 teaspoon salt to a boil in a covered 12-inch skillet over medium-high heat. Reduce the heat to medium-low and cook the quinoa until just tender, about 10 minutes. (Can be covered and refrigerated several days or frozen for several months.)

COOKED WHITE RICE

Makes 7 cups

2 cups medium- or long-grain white rice, any variety
Table salt

Bring 3 cups water, the rice, and 1 teaspoon salt to a boil in a large covered saucepan. Reduce the heat to low and simmer, covered, until the water has evaporated and the rice is fully cooked, about 15 minutes. Remove from the heat and let stand, covered, 5 minutes longer. (Can be covered and refrigerated for several days or frozen for several months.)

COOKED BROWN RICE

Makes 5 cups

If you don't have time to soak brown rice, bring 4 cups water, 2 cups rice, and 1 teaspoon salt to a simmer in a 5- to 6-quart Dutch oven or large saucepan. Cover and cook over medium-low heat until tender, about 45 minutes.

1 pound (2½ cups) long- or short-grain brown rice
Table salt

1. Soak the rice at room temperature in 6 cups water and 1 tablespoon salt for at least 4 and up to 24 hours.

2. Drain and turn the rice into a 12-inch skillet with 3 cups of water and ½ teaspoon salt. Cover and bring to a boil over medium-high heat. Reduce the heat to medium-low and simmer, covered, until tender, about 20 minutes. (Can be covered and refrigerated for several days or frozen for several months.)

A Container of Roasted Nuts

You can toast small quantities of nuts on the stovetop on the fly, but it requires low heat and patience or medium heat and vigilance. Roasting a batch in the oven keeps the process hands-off and foolproof. Plus, you can roast larger quantities of nuts, so that when you need them, you've got them on hand. Roasting nuts at 325°F takes a little more time than at 350°F, but at that temperature it's near impossible to burn them.

HOW TO ROAST ANY NUT

Makes 2 cups

---

2 cups nuts (whole or slivered almonds, walnuts, pecans, cashews, or skinned hazelnuts)

---

1. Adjust the oven rack to lower-middle position and heat the oven to 325°F.

2. Spread the nuts onto a 13 × 9-inch rimmed baking sheet. Bake until fragrant and golden, 7 to 12 minutes, depending on the size of the nut. (Can be stored in a covered container for several weeks or frozen for several months.)

SMOKY PEPITAS

Makes 2 cups

Flavored with smoky paprika, these little seeds pack a ton of flavor and are great for eating out of hand. They also enliven just about any soup, salad, or vegetable you sprinkle them on.

---

2 teaspoons olive oil

1 teaspoon pimentón (smoked paprika)

½ teaspoon kosher salt

¼ teaspoon cayenne pepper

2 cups pepitas (hulled pumpkin seeds)

---

1. Adjust the oven rack to the lower-middle position and heat the oven to 325°F.

2. Mix the oil, pimentón, salt, and cayenne in a medium bowl.

3. Spread the pepitas on a rimmed baking sheet and bake until fragrant and golden, about 10 minutes. Turn the hot pumpkin seeds into the pimentón mixture and toss to coat. (Can be stored in a jar for several weeks.)

A Little Cooked Meat
Goes a Long Way

You're likely to spy bacon or prosciutto bits or sausage crumbles in my fridge. Having any one of these tasty bits on hand is a great way to transform a carton of eggs, an ordinary salad, bowl of grains, or pizza into an extraordinary main course. Sprinkled on top of a bowl of soup or pasta, bacon and prosciutto bits add delightful texture and flavor. It's also one of the best ways I know to make a little meat go a long way.

BACON BITS

Makes a generous 1 cup

1 pound thick-sliced bacon, cut into 1-inch pieces

Place the bacon in a 12-inch skillet and cook over medium-high heat, stirring frequently, until the fat has rendered and the bacon is crisp, about 10 minutes. With a slotted spoon, transfer the bacon from the drippings to paper towels to drain. Discard the drippings or reserve them for another use. (Can be wrapped in foil and stored at room temperature for several days, refrigerated for a couple of weeks, or frozen for several months.)

PROSCIUTTO CRISPS

Makes a generous 1 cup

¼ cup olive oil

12 thin slices (about 6 ounces) prosciutto, sliced crosswise into narrow strips and more or less separated

---

Heat the oil in a large skillet over medium heat. Add the prosciutto and fry, stirring frequently, until frizzled and slightly darker in color, about 5 minutes. Drain on paper towels. (Can be wrapped in foil and stored at room temperature for several days, refrigerated for a couple of weeks, or frozen for several months.) Use the flavored oil for sautéing or drizzling.

SAUSAGE CRUMBLES

Makes scant 3 cups

Having a little cooked sausage in the fridge may be just the ingredient to inspire you to make a quick pot of soup, a skillet frittata, a couple of pizzas, or a big bowl of pasta. It only takes a few minutes to sauté it up, and it eliminates a step on nights when every minute counts.

---

1 pound fresh pork, chicken, or turkey sausage (if using links, remove sausage from casings)

Break up the sausage into a 12-inch skillet over medium-high heat. Cook, stirring constantly, until the sausage loses its raw color, 3 to 4 minutes. Transfer with a slotted spoon to paper towels. (Can be refrigerated in a covered container for a week or frozen for several months.)

A Couple of Quarts
of Bone Broth

You can always use straight cartoned broth to make soups and sauces, but bones add luxurious body and rich, homemade flavor you just don't get with the store-bought stuff—especially when it only takes a little time (and virtually no effort) to make an ingredient with real value. The Hearty Main Course Soups on pages 89 to 93 are filled with meats, vegetables, and starch, so they aren't dependent on homemade broth to taste rich and satisfying. The simple soup recipes that follow the ones for Ham Broth and Beef Bone Broth are for when you have homemade broth and you want it to shine.

QUICK ROAST CHICKEN BROTH

The first thing I do when I get a couple of rotisserie chickens home is pull off the breast meat and legs and thighs, reserving the breasts for another meal and gussying up the legs and thighs for dinner ("Two Chickens, Three Dinners!" page 216). The rest of the bones and skin go into a pot to which I add a carton of broth and 1½ quarts water, and bring to a simmer over medium-low heat. After dinner, I add the leg/thigh bones to the pot and let the broth continue to simmer for a half hour or so. I cool the broth overnight and strain it the next morning. If caramelized onions are my "culinary gold," then homemade chicken broth is my "pot of gold." (See pages 225–227 for more details and recipes on how to use the homemade broth.)

SIMPLE, FLAVORFUL BEEF BONE BROTH

Good chicken broth is easy to buy and easy to make. Good store-bought beef broth is virtually nonexistent. Homemade beef broth takes a little effort, but if you can brown a couple of meaty beef shanks, boost their flavor with red wine, and enrich them with store-bought chicken broth, it's worth it.

RICH HAM BROTH

I look for opportunities to buy a spiral-cut ham—not so much for the meat as for the bone, since I'm never more excited about making soup than when I've got broth made from a ham bone. When there's not a ham bone to be had, you can use a couple of meaty hocks, and if they're not especially meaty, add a small chunk of ham to make up the difference.

HAM BROTH

Makes about 2 quarts

You can use half the ham and broth to create one of the two soups on the following pages. Or use it to make a Hearty Main Course Soup (page 89); you could also double the main course soup recipe and use all the broth and meat.

---

1 meaty ham bone or 2 large meaty ham hocks (2 to 3 pounds)

1 quart chicken broth

---

1. Combine the ham bone, broth, and 6 cups water in a Dutch oven or large pot. Bring to a boil over medium-high heat. Reduce the heat to medium-low and simmer until the bones and skin have released their flavor and the meat is tender, about 1½ hours. Remove from the heat and let stand until warm.

2. Remove and reserve the meat for soup, shredding it into bite-size pieces. Pour the broth into a large covered container, adding water, if necessary, to equal 2 quarts. (Can be refrigerated for at least a week and frozen for several months.) Before using the broth, remove the congealed fat, which can be used, if you like, to sauté soup vegetables (see the following soups).

BLACK BEAN–HOMINY SOUP

Makes about 2 quarts (serves 4)

If you can't find hominy, substitute corn, and if you love hominy as much as I do, make the soup with all hominy! If serving this soup to kids, go with the smaller amount of pepper flakes (or omit them).

2 tablespoons olive oil or ham drippings (see Note)

1 large onion, cut into medium dice

2 teaspoons ground cumin

1 teaspoon dried thyme

¼ to ½ teaspoon red pepper flakes

1 quart Ham Broth (page 66)

Shredded ham (half the amount from Ham Broth)

1 can (15 to 16 ounces) black beans, drained and rinsed

1 can (15 to 16 ounces) hominy, drained

1 can (14.5 ounces) diced tomatoes

¼ cup chopped fresh cilantro (optional)

Salt and ground black pepper

Heat the oil or drippings in a large pot over medium-high heat. Add the onion and sauté until tender. Add the cumin, thyme, pepper flakes, broth, ham, black beans, hominy, and tomatoes. Bring to a simmer, reduce the heat to medium-low, and cook, partially covered, about 15 minutes to blend the flavors. Stir in the cilantro (if using), adjust the seasonings, including salt and pepper to taste. Serve.

Note: Save the congealed fat from the ham broth to use here, if you like.

HAM–WHITE BEAN SOUP

Make a generous 2 quarts (serves 4)

2 tablespoons olive oil or ham drippings (see Note)

1 large onion, cut into medium dice

2 celery stalks, cut into medium dice

2 carrots, cut into medium dice

1 teaspoon dried thyme

1 quart Ham Broth (page 66)

Shredded ham (half the amount from Ham Broth)

4 cups cooked white beans, any kind, or 3 cans (15 to 16 ounces each), drained

Salt and ground black pepper

Heat the oil or drippings in a large pot over medium-high heat. Add the onion, celery, and carrots and sauté until tender. Add the thyme, broth, ham, and beans. Bring to a simmer, reduce the heat to medium-low, and cook, partially covered, for about 15 minutes to blend the flavors. Adjust the seasonings, including salt and pepper to taste. Serve.

Note: Save the congealed fat from the ham broth to use here. Pickled Pink Onions (page 53) are nice on top of the soup. Or top with chopped red onion and drizzle with red wine vinegar as an alternative.

BEEF BONE BROTH

Makes 2 quarts

You can use half the beef and broth to make The Simplest Beef Barley Soup. Or use it to create a Hearty Main Course Soup (page 89); you could also double the main course soup recipe or The Simplest Beef Barley Soup and use all the broth and meat.

---

2 thick, meaty beef shanks (2 to 2 ½ pounds)

Olive oil

Salt and ground black pepper

1 cup red wine

2 quarts chicken broth

---

1. Heat a soup kettle over medium-high heat. Coat both sides of each shank with a little olive oil and season with salt and pepper. Place the shanks in the hot pot and sear, turning only once about halfway through, until well browned on both sides, 8 to 10 minutes total. Add the wine and cook for a minute or so to intensify the flavor. Add the broth and 2 cups water. Bring to a simmer, skimming the foam. Reduce the heat to medium-low and simmer, partially covered, until the meat is tender, about 2 hours.

2. Remove from the heat and let stand until warm. Remove the meat and shred it, discarding the fat and bones, and reserve it for soup. Pour the broth into a 2-quart measuring cup, adding water, if necessary, to equal 2 quarts. (Can be refrigerated at least a week and frozen for several months.) Remove the congealed drippings before using (and save them for sautéing the soup vegetables).

THE SIMPLEST BEEF BARLEY SOUP

Makes a generous 2 quarts (serves 4)

---

2 tablespoons olive oil or beef drippings (see Note)

1 large onion, cut into medium dice

1 teaspoon dried thyme leaves

1 quart Beef Bone Broth

Shredded shank meat (half the amount from Beef Bone Broth)

3 cups cooked barley (page 60)

¼ cup chopped fresh parsley or dill

Salt and ground black pepper

Balsamic vinegar, for drizzling (optional)

Heat the oil or drippings in a large pot over medium-high heat. Add the onion and sauté until tender. Add the thyme, broth, meat, and barley and bring to a simmer. Reduce the heat to medium-low and continue to simmer for about 10 minutes to blend the flavors. Stir in the parsley or dill. Adjust seasonings, including salt and pepper to taste. Serve, drizzled with balsamic vinegar, if you like.

Note: Save the congealed fat from the beef broth to use here, if you like.

A Loaf of Bread

I've been making bread on and off in the food processor for nearly two decades. Making bread in this way makes it nearly impossible to say you don't have time. If you've got 5 minutes, you can make the dough. If you've got another 5 minutes, you can form the loaves. And if you've got a couple of hours of unattended time while the dough rises and the loaves bake, then you've got time to make bread.

The fact is, if there's homemade bread on the table, it almost doesn't matter what else you serve. It's a special meal. One more point: This recipe makes two nice bread rounds. You'll spend ten dollars on loaves of this quality at the grocery store or bakery. I buy bulk flour, yeast, and salt at Costco. Ingredients for those same two loaves cost me under 60 cents!

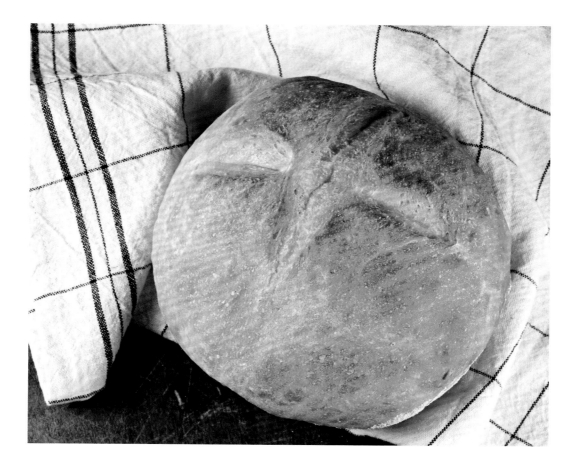

DAILY BREAD

Makes 2 loaves

If you've got an electric oven and you want a better crust on the bread, pour a cup of water onto the oven floor just before adding the loaves (do not do this if you have a gas stove).

⅓ cup tepid water plus 1 ⅓ cups room temperature water

2 teaspoons active dry yeast

4 cups bread flour or unbleached all-purpose flour

2 teaspoons table salt

Cornmeal, for the pan

---

1. Measure the ⅓ cup tepid water in a 2-cup measuring cup. Whisk the yeast into the water. Let stand until foamy, a couple of minutes. Add the remaining 1⅓ cups water to bring the level up to 1⅔ cups.

2. Meanwhile, pulse the flour and salt in a large food processor fitted with the steel blade. Pour the liquid ingredients over the flour and process to form a rough, soft ball. If the dough does not come together, add additional water, a couple of teaspoons at a time. Continue to machine-knead the dough until smooth, about 30 seconds longer.

3. Turn the dough onto a floured surface and knead a few seconds to form a smooth ball. Coat a large bowl with cooking spray, add the dough, and cover with a damp kitchen towel. Let it rise to double in size, about 2 hours.

4. Dump the dough onto a lightly floured surface. Using a chef's knife or a metal dough scraper, halve the dough and form each portion into a ball. Arrange them on a cornmeal-coated 18 × 12-inch rimmed baking sheet. Cover with a damp kitchen towel and let stand until almost double in size, about 45 minutes.

5. Meanwhile, adjust the oven rack to the lowest position and heat the oven to 450°F.

6. With a sharp knife, quickly and decisively cut a cross into each loaf. Place the pan of bread into the hot oven and increase the oven temperature to 500°F. Bake, rotating the baking sheet from back to front after about 15 minutes, until golden brown, about 20 minutes. Transfer to a wire rack to cool. (Can be stored in a 1-gallon zipper-lock bag at room temperature for a couple of days or frozen for several months.)

Loaded Frittata

Frittatas and omelets are great for breakfast and brunch
but a little light for dinner. Enter the Spanish *tortilla*.
Chock-full of potatoes and onions with egg as a mere binder,
this hearty dish, served hot or room temperature, is
substantial fare. I've taken inspiration from the
Spanish *tortilla* and created the Loaded Frittata. In addition
to the *tortilla*'s potatoes and onions, I've added
colorful seasonal vegetables and a little meat and cheese
for a satisfying complete meal.

Loaded Frittata Formula

The formula for the frittata is one of the easiest to follow in this book: 6 to 7 eggs form the base of a dish that can incorporate practically any combination of protein and vegetables you have on hand—from seasonal favorites to extra ingredients left over from other recipes.

VEGETABLES: ½ Pound

Regardless of the ½ pound of vegetables you choose, there is an additional ½ pound of potatoes (a firm vegetable) and ½ pound of onions (a tender vegetable) that are constants in this Loaded Frittata.

You can choose ½ pound of vegetables from either of the categories below. If you choose firm vegetables like broccoli or tough greens like kale, you steam them with the potatoes. If you choose tender vegetables like mushrooms or tender greens like spinach, you sauté them with the onions. As long as you have a total of ½ pound of vegetables, you can even mix it up and choose vegetables from each category!

Because this egg dish is ingredient-dense, you'll need to stagger the cooking. The first step is to cook the potatoes (see step 1 of Loaded Frittata, page 79). This is also when you would add any firm vegetables or hardy greens, which get steamed when the potato is steamed. So that the vegetables steam quickly, cut the firm ones into a small dice or coarsely chop the greens. After steaming, the vegetables are put to the side.

FIRM VEGETABLES/HARDY GREENS

- **Asparagus:** Snap off tough ends and cut into 1-inch lengths (thinly slice thick asparagus spears lengthwise).

- **Cauliflower or broccoli:** Cut into small florets. (Peel and thinly slice any broccoli stems.)

- **Winter squash:** Peel, seed, and cut into small chunks.

- **Brussels sprouts:** Trim, halve small ones, and cut medium and large ones into thick slices.

- **Kale, collards, turnip greens, or broccoli rabe:** Wash, stem, coarsely chop, and massage greens with a couple of teaspoons of olive oil. (The ½ pound greens will measure about 8 packed cups before massaging.)

If you choose one of these tender vegetables or greens, add it once the meat has browned, and you begin to sauté the onion (see step 5 of Loaded Frittata, page 79).

- **Bell peppers:** Cut into small dice.
- **Zucchini or yellow squash:** Cut into small dice.
- **Mushrooms (baby bellas, aka cremini, or domestic whites):** Slice.
- **Cherry or grape tomatoes:** Halve and salt lightly. Because the tomatoes break down quickly, do not cook them with the onion; simply toss them with a tablespoon of olive oil and add them to the skillet once the onion has softened.
- **Fennel:** Trim stalks and fronds, halve, core, and cut into small dice.
- **Baby spinach or arugula:** No prep.
- **Beet greens and Swiss chard:** Thoroughly wash, stem, chop leaves coarsely.
- **Artichoke hearts (9-ounce box frozen, thawed, or 14-ounce can, drained):** Quarter.
- **Frozen corn:** Thaw.

PROTEIN: ½ Pound

After the potatoes and vegetables are on a plate, return the skillet to medium-high to cook one of the meats below.

- **Sliced bacon:** Cut into medium dice. If using bacon, no need to add oil as it will generate its own. In fact, 8 ounces of bacon will likely render more fat than you need, so once the bacon has fried, tilt the pan and spoon off all but a couple of tablespoons.
- **Bulk pork or poultry sausage of any kind (if using links, remove from casings):** Break into small pieces. Fry bulk sausage until it loses its raw color.
- **Cured or smoked pork or poultry sausage links of any kind:** Cut into small dice and sauté until brown.
- **Thick-sliced ham, Canadian bacon, or corned beef:** Cut into small dice and sauté until brown.
- **Hot-smoked salmon:** Break into small pieces. No need to sauté smoked salmon. Just add it to the skillet after the tender vegetables have sautéed.
- **Canned chickpeas:** Drain.

CHEESE: 3 to 4 Ounces

While the vegetables cook, select and grate the cheese. Divide it—no need to measure accurately—tossing a handful into the eggs and saving the remaining handful to sprinkle over the top of the frittata.

Just about any crumbled or grated cheese you've got in your drawer will work, but here are some obvious choices. I tend to go for tangy ones like extra-sharp Cheddar and pepper Jack.

- **Crumbled:** goat or feta
- **Grated:** extra-sharp Cheddar, Gruyère, provolone, Fontina, Swiss, pepper Jack

DRIED HERBS/FRESH HERBS (Pick 1, Optional)

While you're adding the cheese to the eggs, sprinkle in herbs—dried or fresh.
Here are some obvious choices:

- 1 teaspoon dried thyme, oregano, dill, or tarragon (or 1 tablespoon minced fresh)
- 1 teaspoon dried basil leaves (or ¼ cup chopped fresh)
- 2 tablespoons chopped fresh parsley or cilantro

TIPS AND TRICKS

- Omit the meat by substituting ½ pound of another vegetable.
- When the frittata emerges from the oven, it may stick a bit to the pan—especially if you're making it with egg whites or egg substitute. Eventually the steam from the eggs will cause the frittata to loosen from the pan. If you don't want to wait, just cut the frittata into wedges in the pan with a spatula or other tool that will not damage the skillet's surface.

LOADED FRITTATA

Serves 4 to 6

½ pound potatoes (any kind, including sweet), peeled if you like, and cut into small dice

2 tablespoons olive oil

Salt and ground black pepper

½ pound prepared **Firm Vegetables/Hardy Greens** (see page 75) and/or **Tender Vegetables/Tender Greens** (see page 76)

½ pound **Protein** (see page 76)

½ pound onion (1 medium-large), cut into small dice

6 to 7 large eggs, beaten, or 1½ cups egg substitute or egg whites

3 to 4 ounces grated or crumbled **Cheese** (see page 77)

Herb, dried and/or fresh (optional; see page 77)

1. Adjust the oven rack to the upper position and turn the broiler to high.

2. Set a 12-inch heavy-bottomed ovenproof nonstick skillet over low heat.

3. Add the potatoes to the skillet along with ½ cup water, 2 teaspoons oil, and a sprinkling of salt. If using a **Firm Vegetable/Hardy Green,** add it now. Increase the heat to high, cover the skillet, and heat until the water starts to steam. Continue to cook the vegetable(s) until just tender, about 5 minutes (see page 47). Transfer to a plate, scraping as much of the potato starch from the skillet bottom as possible.

4. Return the skillet to medium-high heat. Add another 2 teaspoons oil and the **Protein.** Cook until browned, 4 to 5 minutes. (If using bacon, no need to add oil. Fry it until the fat has rendered and spoon off all but 2 tablespoons of renderings.)

5. Add another 2 teaspoons oil and the onion. If using a **Tender Vegetable/Tender Green,** add it now, giving the onion a bit of a head start. Sauté until the vegetables are tender, 4 to 5 minutes.

6. Season the eggs lightly with salt and pepper and whisk in half the **Cheese** and the **Herb** (if using).

7. Return the potatoes (and any firm vegetables) to the skillet and shake to evenly distribute. Set over low heat, drizzle in the egg mixture, and sprinkle on the remaining cheese. Transfer the pan to the oven and broil until the eggs are puffed and the cheese has melted, 3 to 5 minutes. Remove the frittata from the oven and let rest for a few minutes. Use a plastic spatula to cut the frittata into 4 to 6 wedges and serve.

Tomato-Basil Loaded Frittata with Italian Sausage

Protein: bulk Italian sausage
**Tender Vegetables/
Tender Greens:** tomatoes
Cheese: sharp Cheddar
Herb: fresh basil

Ham and Asparagus Loaded Frittata with Tarragon and Gruyère

**Firm Vegetables/
Hardy Greens:** asparagus
Protein: ham
Cheese: Gruyère
Herb: dried or fresh tarragon

Bacon-Kale Loaded Frittata with Sharp Cheddar

**Firm Vegetables/
Hardy Greens:** kale
Protein: bacon
Cheese: sharp Cheddar
Herb: dried oregano

Corn-Tomato Loaded Frittata with Pepper Jack

Here I've opted to omit the meat and use 2 vegetables instead.

**Tender Vegetables/
Tender Greens:** ½ pound each corn and tomatoes
Cheese: pepper Jack
Herb: cilantro

Greek Loaded Frittata with Spinach, Feta, and Dill

**Tender Vegetables/
Tender Greens:** spinach
Protein: ham
Cheese: feta
Herb: dill

Corned Beef Loaded Frittata

Protein: corned beef
**Tender Vegetables/
Tender Greens:** red bell pepper
Cheese: Swiss
Herb: dried thyme

Frittata with Sausage, Fennel, and Fontina

Protein: Italian sausage
**Tender Vegetables/
Tender Greens:** fennel
Cheese: Fontina
Herb: parsley

Frittata with Chickpeas and Rabe

**Firm Vegetables/
Hardy Greens:** broccoli rabe
Protein: chickpeas
Cheese: pepper Jack
Herb: parsley

At a Glance

LOADED FRITTATA

1. Internalize the formula: ½ pound each potatoes, vegetables, protein, and onion; 1½ cups eggs; 3 to 4 ounces cheese; a little oil, and herbs.

2. Know the technique: Steam the potatoes along with the firm vegetables/hardy greens (if using) in a large skillet, then turn them onto a plate.

3. Cook the protein. Sauté the onion along with the tender vegetables/tender greens (if using).

4. Return the potato mixture to the skillet and shake to evenly distribute.

5. Add the eggs and cheese; top with the remaining cheese and herbs and broil.

Soup for Supper

Soup is a universal comfort food, and in this chapter, there are two quick, simple soup formulas—one chunky, hearty, and stew-like and the other, smooth, creamy, and stick-to-your ribs. Both can be made in under a half hour, and you can tailor the ingredient lists to appeal to your crowd.

Hearty Main Course Soup Formula

This formula is easy to internalize: 1 pound protein, 1 pound vegetables, 1 quart broth, 1 onion, 1 can tomatoes, a starch (potatoes, rice, pasta, beans), and herbs, spices, and/or flavorings. The technique is simple, too: Sauté an onion until softened, add the remaining ingredients, bring it to a simmer, cook for about 20 minutes, and serve it up. There are a few logical exceptions, but better to know a formula and remember the exceptions than not to know a formula at all.

PROTEIN: 1 Pound

When making quick supper soups, buy cuts that cook quickly like the following. Depending on the cut, the preparation and cooking will vary slightly. Some cuts you simply add straight to the pot, either at the beginning with all the other ingredients or at the very end. Others you add at the beginning but fish out and shred or cut into bite-size pieces. Still others you brown in the pot before sautéing the onion.

JUST ADD AS IS

- **Ham:** Cube or shred and add with the broth.
- **Smoked and cured sausages of any kind:** Slice and add with the broth.
- **Fish fillets:** Add with the broth and use a spatula to flake them as they cook.
- **Peeled shrimp:** If large, cut into bite-size pieces and drop into the soup the last few minutes of cooking.
- **Bay scallops:** Drop into the soup the last few minutes of cooking.

BROWN AND SLICE

- **Fresh sausages of any kind:** Brown in the hot soup pot (no need to fully cook) before sautéing the onion. Slice and add with the broth. Or remove the raw sausage from its casing and sauté, then add the onion. No need to remove it from the pot.

SIMMER AND SHRED

- **Boneless, skinless chicken breasts:** Cut into thirds crosswise, add with the broth, remove the last few minutes of cooking, shred with two forks, and return to the soup.
- **Boneless, skinless chicken thighs:** Add with the broth, remove the last few minutes of cooking, shred with two forks, and return to the soup.
- **Pork tenderloin:** Cut crosswise into 2- to 3-inch chunks, add with the broth, remove the last few minutes of cooking, shred with two forks, and return to the soup.

VEGETABLES: 1 Pound

Do certain vegetables go with certain meats? Some combinations are a natural—sausage with cabbage and potatoes or chicken with carrots and peas—but there's not a bad match between any of the suggested soup vegetables and meats, poultry, or fish.

COMMON SOUP VEGETABLES

- **Asparagus:** Snap off tough ends and cut into 1-inch lengths (halve thick asparagus spears lengthwise).

- **Broccoli or cauliflower:** Cut into small florets. For broccoli stalks, remove the tough outer peel and slice ¼ inch thick. Or, buy packaged florets.

- **Brussels sprouts:** Trim root end and halve lengthwise, if small. Cut into thick slices, if large.

- **Turnips, rutabagas, and all winter squash:** Peel and cut into bite-size chunks (seed winter squash).

- **Cabbage:** Halve, core, and thinly slice.

- **Carrots or celery:** Cut into medium dice (peel carrots).

- **Green beans:** Trim ends and snap into bite-size pieces.

- **Green peas, frozen:** No prep.

- **Beet, turnip, collard, and mustard greens, Swiss chard, kale, and large spinach:** Stem, wash, and coarsely chop (or buy bagged prepared greens).

- **Bok choy:** Thinly slice crisp edible stem; coarsely chop leaves.

- **Broccoli rabe:** Peel stems, if tough, then coarsely chop leaves and stems.

- **Curly endive and escarole:** Trim root end, wash, and coarsely chop.

- **Baby spinach:** No prep (just make sure they're clean).

- **Bell peppers:** Stem, seed, and cut into small dice.

- **Fennel:** Trim the fronds and stalks and reserve fronds. Halve, core, and cut into small dice.

- **Leeks:** Trim off the tough dark green tops and discard. Quarter lengthwise, then cut crosswise into ½-inch-thick slices. Wash thoroughly.

- **Mushrooms, domestic white and baby bella:** Trim stem ends, rinse, and slice.

- **Yellow squash and zucchini:** Trim and cut into small dice.

STARCH

Unless you're using potatoes—an easy-to-remember 1 pound—the starch options for the soup formula aren't as neat and tidy. See options below.

If you like, you can add two different starches to the soup. For example, ½ pound potatoes plus 1 can beans, or 1 cup corn plus 1 can beans. Also, if you have cooked pasta or rice, you can use it instead of raw. Figure a generous 1½ cups cooked pasta or ¾ cup cooked rice, and add it to the soup during the last few minutes of cooking.

- 1 pound potatoes, any kind, diced
- 2 cans (15 to 16 ounces each) beans or hominy, drained
- 2 cups fresh or frozen corn
- 1½ cups wide or extra-wide egg noodles or ¾ cup bite-size pasta
- ⅓ cup long-grain white rice

FLAVORINGS

Herbs and spices add flavor and character to a soup. While this list of flavorings is not comprehensive, it includes most of the common herbs and spices and is enough to get you comfortable with flavoring your own soup. Add dried herbs and woody fresh herbs, such as rosemary and thyme, as well as spices at the beginning with the broth. Add soft fresh herbs and other flavorings during the last few minutes of cooking.

DRIED HERBS, WOODY FRESH HERBS, AND SPICES

- 1 tablespoon curry powder or garam masala
- 2 teaspoons minced fresh rosemary, thyme, or chopped fennel seeds
- 1 teaspoon dried thyme, basil, or tarragon, or ground cumin or coriander
- ½ teaspoon dried oregano or caraway seeds
- ¼ teaspoon hot red pepper flakes

FRESH HERBS AND FLAVORINGS

- ¼ cup chopped fresh basil
- 2 tablespoons chopped fresh parsley, cilantro, or mint, or lemon or lime juice
- 1 tablespoon chopped fresh dill or tarragon
- 1 teaspoon finely grated lemon zest

HEARTY MAIN COURSE SOUP

Makes 4 generous servings

---

2 tablespoons olive oil

1 large onion, chopped

1 pound prepared **Vegetables** (see page 86)

1 pound **Protein** (prepared as directed; see page 85)

1 pound **Starch** (see page 87)

1 can (14.5 ounces) tomatoes, diced or crushed, your choice (occasionally optional)

1 quart chicken broth (or fish or seafood broth if using fish, shrimp, or scallops)

Flavorings (see Note)

Salt and ground black pepper

Heat the oil in a large pot over medium-high heat. Add the onion and sauté to soften slightly, 4 to 5 minutes. Add the **Vegetables, Protein** (except shrimp and scallops, which are added during the last 5 minutes of cooking), **Starch,** tomatoes, broth, and **Flavorings** (if using dried herbs, woody fresh herbs, or spices). Bring to a simmer, reduce the heat to medium-low, and simmer, partially covered, until the vegetables are tender and the flavors have blended, 15 to 20 minutes. Add any **Flavorings** and extra broth or water if needed: The soup should be thick, but juicy. Adjust seasonings, including salt and pepper to taste. Serve.

Note: Flavorings can be dried or fresh herbs, spices, or other flavorings (such as citrus juice or zest).

See Suggestions (page 87) for ideas and general guidelines.

TIPS AND TRICKS

- If you prefer the green soup vegetables brightly colored rather than fully cooked, add them during the last 5 minutes of cooking rather than with the rest of the vegetables.

- If you prefer the green soup vegetables fully cooked but want bright color, add a handful of chopped fresh herbs, such as parsley, basil, or cilantro, at the end of cooking.

- To make the soup vegetarian, substitute vegetable broth for chicken broth, omit the meat, and add a second starch (grains, beans, or potatoes).

- To decrease the amount of meat and use it just as flavoring, increase the vegetables from 1 to 1½ pounds and decrease the meat from 1 pound to ½ pound.

- Vegetable weights don't need to be exact, but allow a little more than a pound, so by the time you've trimmed them, you've got close to a pound.

- Time permitting, boost a shrimp-based soup's flavor by simmering the shrimp shells in some of the broth for a few minutes. Strain them out before adding the broth to the soup.

- For quicker chicken soup, use 2 to 3 cups shredded rotisserie chicken instead of chicken breasts or thighs.

Sausage, White Bean,
and Escarole Soup

Fish Soup *with* Cabbage *and* Potatoes

Chicken Vegetable Soup *with* Wide Noodles

Ham and Potato Soup with Leeks and Peas

Protein: ham chunk, shredded or diced
Vegetables: 2 small leeks, 2 small carrots, ¾ cup frozen green peas
Starch: red potatoes
Flavorings: 1 teaspoon dried thyme

Follow Hearty Main Course Soup technique, omitting tomatoes.

Sausage, White Bean, and Escarole Soup

Ham is equally good in this soup. Remember to add woody fresh herbs like rosemary and thyme at the beginning with the broth rather than at the end like other fresh herbs.

Protein: mild or hot Italian sausage links
Vegetables: ½ medium head escarole, 2 medium carrots
Starch: cannellini beans
Flavorings: 2 teaspoons minced fresh rosemary

Sausage Soup with Mushrooms, Zucchini, and Chickpeas

Protein: mild or hot Italian sausage links
Vegetables: ½ pound white mushrooms, 1 medium zucchini
Starch: chickpeas
Flavorings: 1 teaspoon ground cumin

Follow Hearty Main Course Soup technique, tossing the mushrooms into the sautéing onions, if there's time.

Sausage Soup with Spinach, Cauliflower, and Noodles

Protein: mild or hot Italian sausage links
Vegetables: ½ pound cauliflower florets, ½ pound spinach
Starch: bite-size pasta, such as macaroni or bow ties
Flavorings: 1 teaspoon dried or ¼ cup chopped fresh basil

Pork Soup with Hominy and Peppers

This soup is equally good made with ham or chicken. Serve with a squeeze of lime, tortilla chips, and guacamole.

Protein: pork tenderloin
Vegetables: 1 large bell pepper, 1 medium zucchini or yellow squash
Starch: hominy
Flavorings: 2 tablespoons chopped fresh cilantro

Chicken Vegetable Soup with Wide Noodles

If you add the peas at the beginning, freshen the color by stirring in a couple of tablespoons of chopped fresh parsley at the end. Or, add the peas the last few minutes of cooking. Also, remember you can use shredded rotisserie chicken in place of the thighs or breasts.

Protein: boneless, skinless chicken thighs or breasts
Vegetables: 2 medium carrots, 2 medium celery stalks, ¾ cup frozen green peas
Starch: wide egg noodles
Flavorings: 1 teaspoon dried thyme

Follow Hearty Main Course Soup technique, omitting tomatoes.

Lemon Chicken Soup with Spinach and Rice

Protein: boneless, skinless chicken thighs or breasts
Vegetables: 10 ounces baby spinach, 1 medium zucchini
Starch: white rice
Flavorings: 2 tablespoons lemon juice, 1 tablespoon chopped fresh dill

Follow Hearty Main Course Soup technique, adding lemon juice and dill to the finished soup.

Curried Chicken Soup with Sweet Potatoes, Cauliflower, and Spinach

Here, I use half chickpeas and half potatoes to exemplify how two starches can work in the same soup. If you don't have one or the other, simply double the amount of the one you've got.

Protein: boneless, skinless chicken thighs
Vegetables: cauliflower florets and baby spinach—you decide how much of each
Starch: 1 sweet potato (8 ounces) and 1 can chickpeas
Flavorings: 1 tablespoon curry powder, 2 tablespoons chopped fresh cilantro

Follow Hearty Main Course Soup technique, adding the curry powder to the broth and topping the finished soup with the cilantro.

Fish Soup with Cabbage and Potatoes

Remember to use fish or seafood broth here. Or, if you prefer, substitute kielbasa or ham for the fish and eliminate the lemon zest and juice. To brighten the soup before serving, add a little chopped parsley if you have it.

Protein: firm-fleshed white fish, such as halibut, cod, scrod, or haddock
Vegetables: ¼ medium cabbage, 2 medium celery stalks or 1 small fennel bulb
Starch: potatoes
Flavorings: 2 teaspoons finely chopped fennel seeds, ¼ teaspoon red pepper flakes, and 1 teaspoon finely grated lemon zest, 2 tablespoons lemon juice

Follow Hearty Main Course Soup technique, adding the fennel seeds and pepper flakes with the broth and zest and juice to the finished soup.

Gumbo-Style Shrimp Soup

Even better, make this soup with half shrimp and half kielbasa (8 ounces each). You can also reduce rice to ¼ cup and add a can of pinto beans. Remember to use seafood or fish broth here.

Protein: medium shrimp
Vegetables: 1 bell pepper, 2 large celery stalks
Starch: white rice
Flavorings: 2 bay leaves, 2 tablespoons chopped fresh parsley

---

At a Glance

HEARTY MAIN COURSE SOUP

1. Internalize the formula: 1 onion, 1 pound vegetables, 1 pound protein, 1 quart broth, 1 can tomatoes (sometimes optional), a starch, a couple of tablespoons of oil, and flavorings.

2. Know the technique: Sauté the onion, add the vegetables, protein, starch, tomatoes, broth, dried herbs, and/or spices, if using.

3. Bring to a simmer and cook for 15 minutes. Stir in fresh flavorings (if using).

Quick Creamy Pureed Vegetable Soup Formula

Making a creamy vegetable soup is almost as simple as blending a morning smoothie, and even if the pantry is nearly bare, you'll likely have ingredients to make one of them. You'll need a vegetable (it can be as basic as potatoes or carrots), a few garlic cloves, a little olive oil, some broth, a splash of milk, and a seasoning, such as dried or fresh herbs, spices, or zests.

Paired with a hearty salad, pureed soups make a quick weeknight supper. They're also elegant enough to serve as a first course at a nice dinner. In the warmer months these soups can be served chilled as well—just cover and refrigerate until ready to serve.

VEGETABLES: 1 Pound

To make a creamy vegetable soup, you need vegetables that can act as both flavoring and thickener. Tender vegetables like mushrooms, peppers, tomatoes, onions, and summer squash are too moist and require extra thickener to turn into soup. But there are plenty of firm vegetables that will work, and here's the list.

- **Asparagus:** Snap off tough ends and cut into 1-inch lengths (halve thick asparagus spears lengthwise).
- **Broccoli or cauliflower:** Cut into small florets. For broccoli stalks, remove the tough outer peel and slice ¼ inch thick. Or, buy packaged florets.
- **Brussels sprouts:** Trim root end and halve lengthwise.
- **Turnips, rutabagas, beets, sweet potatoes, and all winter squash:** Peel and cut into bite-size chunks (seed winter squash).
- **Cabbage:** Halve, core, and thinly slice.
- **Carrots:** Peel and slice ¼ inch thick, halve large ones lengthwise.
- **Green beans:** Trim ends and snap into bite-size pieces.
- **Any baking or boiling potatoes:** Quarter if small, or cut into bite-size chunks if large. (Scrub potatoes if dirty.)
- **Green peas, frozen:** No prep.

LIQUID: 2 Cups Broth + ½ Cup Milk

Without broth and milk, the blended vegetables would simply be purees. Use broth to reinforce the soup's savoriness and milk to add richness. I prefer evaporated milk in this soup for two reasons. It's shelf stable, which means you don't have to keep perishable specialty milks like half-and-half or cream on hand. Evaporated milk offers the body and richness of heavy cream without the fat and calories.

You can make this soup three ways: with chicken broth and evaporated milk for most tastes, vegetable broth and evaporated milk for vegetarians, or vegetable broth and coconut milk for vegans.

FLAVORINGS

If you use the flavoring suggestions as a guide from the Quick Creamy Pureed Vegetable Soup (page 97) or the Hearty Main Course Soup (page 89) and reduce them by half (for example, 1 tablespoon of curry powder for a Hearty Main Course Soup would be 1½ teaspoons for a Quick Creamy Pureed Vegetable Soup) you'll quickly get comfortable reaching in the spice cabinet and flavoring your own soups.

GARNISHES

Crispy, crunchy garnishes offer textural contrast to the smooth creamy soups.
Here are some to consider:

- Use the **steam-sautéed vegetables** as a natural garnish by simply pulling off a few of the cooked vegetables before adding the broth. Float a few pieces on each bowl of soup.

- **Roasted nuts of any kind** (**walnuts, pecans, almonds, hazelnuts, pine nuts, cashews, macadamia nuts**): Toast ½ cup or less in a small skillet over medium-low heat, shaking the skillet frequently, until fragrant and golden brown. Roast larger quantities of nuts in a 325°F oven until fragrant and golden, 10 to 15 minutes, depending on nut.

- **Toasted seeds** (**pumpkin seeds, sunflower seeds**): Toast ¼ cup or less in a small skillet over medium-low heat, shaking the skillet frequently, until fragrant and golden brown. Roast larger quantities in a 325°F oven until fragrant and golden brown, 8 to 10 minutes.

- **Smoky Pepitas** (page 62)

- **Pickled Pink Onions** (page 53)

- **Bacon Bits** (page 63) or **Prosciutto Crisps** (page 64)

QUICK CREAMY PUREED VEGETABLE SOUP

Makes about 1 quart

½ teaspoon salt

Pinch of red pepper flakes (optional)

Flavorings (see Note)

1 tablespoon olive oil

1 pound prepared **Vegetables** (see page 94)

3 large garlic cloves, minced

2 cups chicken or vegetable broth

½ cup evaporated milk or regular coconut milk

Ground black pepper

Garnishes (optional; see page 95)

1. Mix the salt, pepper flakes (if using), **Flavorings** (if using dried herbs, woody fresh herbs, or spices), oil, and ⅓ cup water in a large skillet. Add the **Vegetables,** cover, and set over high heat. Steam until the vegetables are brightly colored and just tender, 5 to 7 minutes.

2. Uncover, add the garlic, and continue to cook until the liquid evaporates and the vegetables and garlic start to brown, 1 to 2 minutes longer. Add the broth and bring to a full simmer.

3. Transfer the mixture and any **Flavorings** to a blender and puree, adding the milk as it processes. Return the soup to the skillet over medium heat and adjust the seasonings, including pepper to taste. Thin with additional broth or water to your desired thickness. Heat until the soup starts to bubble. Serve with optional **Garnishes.**

Note: This can be dried or fresh herbs, spices, or other flavorings (such as citrus juice or zest). See Suggestions (page 87) for ideas and general guidelines, using half the amount suggested for Hearty Main Course Soup.

TIPS AND TRICKS

- Fresh herbs are added before pureeing the soup. The only fresh herb exceptions are thyme and rosemary. Instead, treat these hearty herbs like dried ones.

- If you like, substitute ½ small onion, chopped, for the garlic, adding it along with the vegetables at the beginning.

- You can substitute other milks for the evaporated milk or coconut milk. The leaner the milk, the more prominent the vegetable flavor; the richer the milk, the more creamy and satisfying the soup.

Creamy Broccoli Soup with Lemon

Vegetable: broccoli
Flavorings: ½ teaspoon finely grated lemon zest
Garnishes: toasted pine nuts

Creamy Butternut Squash Soup with Sage

Vegetable: butternut squash
Flavorings: ½ teaspoon rubbed sage
Garnishes: any chopped candied nut

Creamy Brussels Sprout Soup with Caraway

Vegetable: Brussels sprouts
Flavorings: ¼ teaspoon caraway seeds
Garnishes: chopped toasted walnuts

Curried Sweet Potato Soup

Vegetable: sweet potatoes
Flavorings: 1½ teaspoons curry powder and 3 to 4 cilantro springs
Garnishes: finely diced crisp apple

Creamy Potato Soup with Rosemary

Vegetable: boiling or baking potatoes
Flavorings: 1½ teaspoons minced fresh rosemary
Garnishes: Bacon Bits (page 63)

Creamy Carrot Soup with Ginger

Vegetable: carrots
Flavorings: ½ teaspoon ground ginger
Garnishes: toasted pepitas (hulled pumpkin seeds)

Creamy Turnip Soup with Thyme

Vegetable: turnips
Flavorings: ½ teaspoon dried or 1½ teaspoons minced fresh thyme leaves
Garnishes: Pickled Pink Onions (page 53)

Creamy Asparagus Soup with Tarragon

Vegetable: asparagus
Flavorings: ½ teaspoon dried tarragon and ½ teaspoon finely grated lemon zest
Garnishes: Prosciutto Crisps (page 64)

Creamy Cauliflower Soup with Cumin

Vegetable: cauliflower
Flavorings: ½ teaspoon ground cumin and 3 to 4 sprigs cilantro
Garnishes: toasted pepitas (hulled pumpkin seeds)

At a Glance
QUICK CREAMY PUREED VEGETABLE SOUP

1. Internalize the formula: 1 pound vegetables, 2 cups broth, garlic cloves, ½ cup milk, and flavorings.

2. Know the technique: Steam the vegetables, adding the garlic once the lid is removed.

3. Add the broth and bring to a simmer.

4. Transfer the mixture to a blender and puree, adding the milk as it blends.

5. Return the soup to the skillet and heat, thinning it with additional broth or water, if necessary. Adjust the seasonings and serve.

Hearty Grain and Legume Salads, Warm or Cold

Whether you're an omnivore, vegetarian, or vegan,
legumes and grains appeal to nearly everyone. Vegetable
heavy, these protein-rich salads offer a satisfying
and complete meal to vegetarians and vegans. Omnivores
can enjoy it as is or top the healthful mound with seared
seafood, chicken, pork, or steak.

Hearty Grain and Legume Salad Formula

If you've got cooked grains in the fridge or freezer (see "A Little Mise," page 34) and a can of beans in the pantry, you can make these salads with whatever vegetables and flavorings you've got around. With its 4 cups of legumes and grains, 3 cups of vegetables, and 1 cup of flavorings, there'll nearly always be enough salad for tonight's dinner as well as some for lunch the next day.

COOKED GRAINS AND/OR LEGUMES: 4 Cups (Pick 1, 2, or Even 3)

You can make salads with either all grains or all legumes, but I prefer a mix (about 2 cups each). The recipes for cooking legumes and grains (both here and on pages 59 to 61) produce more than the amount needed for these salads, but they both refrigerate and freeze well, so consider the leftovers your money in the bank—the start of another great meal down the road.

LEGUMES

- **Beans, canned:** Choices are chickpeas, white beans (such as Great Northern, navy, or cannellini), black beans, pinto beans, dark or light kidney beans, black-eyed peas. A 15- to 16-ounce can yields about 1½ cups of drained beans. If using 2 cans beans (3 cups), use only 1 cup grains. If using 1 can beans (1½ cups) use 2½ cups grains.

- **Beans, dried:** See Cooked Beans (page 58) for soaking and cooking instructions.

- **Edamame, green peas, lima beans, frozen:** 12 ounces yields about 2 cups. To thaw, microwave on high power in a microwave-safe covered container for 3 to 4 minutes.

- **Lentils:** Choices are black, brown, or green lentils or lentils du Puy. See Cooked Lentils (page 57) for cooking instructions.

- **Split peas:** See Cooked Split Peas (page 58) for cooking instructions.

GRAINS

- **Barley:** See Cooked Barley (page 60) for cooking instructions.

- **Bulgur:** Pour 1½ cups boiling water over 1½ cups bulgur and 1 teaspoon salt in a medium bowl; cover with plastic wrap and let stand until the water has absorbed and the grains are tender, 15 to 20 minutes. Fluff with a fork. Yields about 4 cups.

- **Corn, frozen:** 12 ounces yields about 2 cups. To thaw, microwave on high power in a microwave-safe container for 3 to 4 minutes. (If using fresh corn, figure a scant cup of kernels per a medium ear. You can use raw or fresh corn kernels.)

- **Couscous, regular:** Pour 1½ cups boiling water over 1½ cups couscous and 1 teaspoon salt in a medium bowl. Cover with plastic wrap and let stand until water has absorbed and grains are tender, 5 to 7 minutes. Fluff with a fork. Yields a generous 4 cups.

- **Couscous, Israeli:** Bring 2 quarts water and 1 tablespoon salt to a boil in a soup kettle. Add 2 cups Israeli couscous and cook, stirring frequently at the beginning, until tender, 8 to 10 minutes. Yields about 2 cups.

- **Farro, pearled:** Soak 1 pound (about 2⅔ cups) farro in 6 cups water and 1 tablespoon salt for at least 4 and up to 24 hours. Drain farro and transfer to a 12-inch skillet. Add 3 cups water and ½ teaspoon salt. Cover and bring to a boil. Reduce the heat to medium-low, and simmer until just tender, about 10 minutes. Yields about 6 cups.

- **Millet:** Soak 1 pound (about 2⅓ cups) millet in 6 cups water and 1 tablespoon salt for at least 4 and up to 24 hours. Drain millet and transfer to a 12-inch skillet. Add 3 cups water and ½ teaspoon salt. Cover and bring to a boil. Reduce the heat to medium-low and cook until almost tender, 6 to 8 minutes. Remove from heat and let stand until the water is absorbed, a couple of minutes longer. Yields about 7 cups.

- **Pasta, bite-size:** The shape determines the yield, but you won't go too far wrong by bringing 2 quarts water and 1 tablespoon salt to a boil in a Dutch oven or soup kettle. Add 8 ounces pasta and, following package times as a guide, cook until just tender. Drain and turn onto a rimmed baking sheet to cool. (Do not run under cold running water. The dressing will help the pasta to separate.)

- **Quinoa:** See Cooked Quinoa (page 61) for cooking instructions.

- **Rice, brown:** You can buy cooked brown rice. For 2 cups you'll need an 8.8-ounce package. If using instant brown rice or quick-cooking brown rice, simply follow the package instructions. To cook regular brown rice (it cooks in just 20 minutes if you remember to soak it) see Cooked Brown Rice (page 61).

- **Rice, white:** You can buy cooked white rice. For 2 cups you'll need an 8.8-ounce package. Unlike instant brown rice, which is toothsome, instant white rice is mushy and not recommended. To cook rice, see Cooked White Rice (page 61).

- **Wheat berries, Kamut, and spelt:** Even with soaking, these grains take the longest to cook of any legumes and grains, so cook a full pound. Freeze the rest. Soak 1 pound (about 2⅓ cups) in 6 cups water and 1 tablespoon salt for at least 4 and up to 24 hours. Drain and transfer to a large pot with 6 cups water and 1 teaspoon salt. Cover and bring to a boil. Reduce the heat to medium-low and cook until the water is nearly absorbed and the grains are tender, 45 minutes to 1 hour. The yield for each grain varies slightly, but figure 5 to 6 cups.

VEGETABLES: 3 Cups (Pick 2 or 3)

Except for root vegetables and winter squash, which taste better cooked, bean and grain salads benefit from the crunch and freshness of raw vegetables. Use any one of the following vegetables in legume and grain salads, figuring 2 to 3 types per salad.

RAW VEGETABLES

- **Asparagus:** Snap off tough ends, into 1-inch lengths, and thinly slice lengthwise.
- **Bean sprouts:** Simply open the plastic bag, rinse, and dump.
- **Bell peppers (any color):** Thinly slice into short strips.
- **Cauliflower or broccoli crowns:** Cut into small bite-size florets. (Thinly slice and peel the broccoli stems.)
- **Brussels sprouts:** Trim and thinly slice.
- **Cabbage:** Halve, core, and thinly slice.
- **Yellow squash, zucchini, carrots, or parsnips:** Coarsely grate or cut into small dice. (Peel carrots and parsnips.)
- **Celery:** Cut into small dice.
- **Cherry or grape tomatoes:** Halve if small, quarter if large. Lightly salt.
- **Cucumbers:** Partially peel (leave stripes of green for color), cut into small dice, and lightly salt.
- **Fennel:** Trim fronds and stalks, then quarter, core, and thinly slice.
- **Green beans, thin or haricot verts:** Trim and cut into bite-size lengths.
- **Mushrooms, white or baby bellas:** Trim stems and thinly slice.
- **Radishes:** Trim, halve if large, and thinly slice.
- **Snow peas or sugar snap peas:** Stem and string, if necessary. Cut into bite-size pieces.
- **Water chestnuts, sliced, canned:** Drain and rinse. One 8-ounce can = 5 ounces drained.

COOKED VEGETABLES

- **Artichoke heart quarters:** Frozen from a 9-ounce box, thawed, or 14-ounce can, drained.
- **Frozen green peas:** Simply thaw.
- **Root vegetables,** such as potatoes, turnips, sweet potatoes, and rutabagas, and winter squash are better cooked. Of course you can roast them (see page 39) and then cut them into a small dice, but if you need them quick, peel and cut them into small dice and steam-sauté them (see page 48). No need to peel regular potatoes, and don't forget to seed the winter squash!

HEARTY GRAIN & LEGUME SALADS

Asian-Flavored Rice *and* **Green Pea Salad** *with* **Bean Sprouts** *and* **Peppers**

Creamy Lentil *and* **Barley Salad** *with* **Broccoli, Carrots,** *and* **Raisins**

Couscous *and* **Chickpea Salad** *with* **Peppers, Zucchini, Apricots,** *and* **Almonds**

Black Bean *and* **Corn Salad** *with* **Cilantro-Lime Dressing**

FLAVORINGS: ½ Cup Each (Pick 1 or 2)

To boost flavor, I frequently choose two flavorings, but if you don't have the time or the ingredients, one is sufficient, in which case you might want to be a little more generous.

- **Bacon Bits** (page 63) or **Prosciutto Crisps** (page 64)
- **Cheese:** Crumbled goat or feta, coarsely grated Parmesan cheese.
- **Dried fruit:** Cranberries, raisins, blueberries, diced apricots, peaches, mango, and dates are especially good.
- **Toasted nuts:** Try pistachios or pine nuts, slivered or sliced almonds, coarsely chopped pecans, walnuts, hazelnuts, or cashews. For a cup or less, toast them in a medium skillet over medium-low heat, stirring them or shaking the pan frequently, until fragrant and shade darker. For more than a cup, see page 62 for roasting instructions.
- **Olives, green or black:** Pit and coarsely chop.
- **Pickles, dill or sweet:** Cut into small dice.
- **Pickled peppers, such as jalapeños or peppadews:** Cut into small dice.
- **Seeds (sesame seeds, hulled pumpkin seeds):** For a cup or less, toast them in a medium skillet over medium-low heat, stirring them or shaking the pan frequently, until fragrant and shade darker. For more than a cup, see page 62 for roasting instructions.
- **Sun-dried tomatoes:** Coarsely chop.

ONION: ½ Cup Sliced

I rarely make a salad without onion, and legume and grains salads are no exception. I like the purple hue and crunch of a red onion, but in more delicate salads, the subtle texture and flavor of scallion works well. But I can't hide my preference for Pickled Pink Onions (page 53). If you've got a jar in the fridge, use them!

DRESSING: 1 Cup

Mild-mannered beans and grains benefit from a punchy dressing. The ones that follow offer the fresh herbaceous-ness of pesto and all the kick of good vinaigrette. After dressing the salad, taste it. It'll likely need salt and pepper, but you may want more acidity, so confidently drizzle the salad with extra vinegar or citrus to your liking.

HERB DRESSING

Makes about 1 cup

1 cup packed parsley, basil, or cilantro (see Note)

2 medium garlic cloves

½ cup extra-virgin olive oil

6 tablespoons vinegar (red wine, white wine, sherry, balsamic), fresh lemon juice, or fresh lime juice

¼ teaspoon red pepper flakes

Salt and ground black pepper

Place all of the ingredients, including a big pinch of salt and several grinds of pepper, in a food processor and blend until smooth. (Can be transferred to a jar and refrigerated for several days.)

Note: You can also use more assertive fresh herbs like dill, mint, or tarragon. But use only ¼ cup of them and balance with ¾ cup parsley, basil, or cilantro.

CREAMY HERB DRESSING

Makes about 1 cup

1 cup packed fresh parsley, cilantro, or basil

2 medium garlic cloves

½ cup mayonnaise

½ cup plain Greek yogurt

4 teaspoons red wine vinegar

4 teaspoons milk

Salt and ground black pepper

Place all of the ingredients, including a big pinch of salt and several grinds of pepper, in a food processor and blend until smooth. (Can be transferred to a jar and refrigerated for several days.)

ASIAN DRESSING

Makes about 1 cup

The garlic and ginger pastes that you find in the produce department work well here.

1 cup packed fresh cilantro leaves (see Note)

½ cup neutral oil, such as canola

2 tablespoons toasted sesame oil

2 tablespoons soy sauce

2 tablespoons rice vinegar

1 tablespoon sugar

2 teaspoons minced garlic

2 teaspoons minced fresh ginger

½ teaspoon red pepper flakes

Place all of the ingredients in a food processor; blend until smooth. (Can be transferred to a jar and refrigerated for several days.)

Note: If you're not a cilantro fan, substitute fresh basil. You can also use a combination of cilantro and mint: Figure ¾ cup cilantro and ¼ cup mint.

- To bulk up any grain and legume salad, add a couple of cups of salad greens just before tossing. Or, serve over a bed of lightly dressed greens.

- Top any legume and grain salad with seared sea scallops, fish steaks, chicken breasts or thighs, pork tenderloin medallions, or steak or a fried egg.

- You can also use fresh fruit in place of some of the vegetables. Think apples and carrots; berries and celery; or fennel, mango, and cucumber.

- To enliven any leftover grain and legume salads, season to taste with additional salt, pepper, and vinegar or lemon juice.

- If you need to save time, toss the salad with ½ cup olive oil and salt and pepper to taste. Drizzle in vinegar to taste, and add a handful of chopped fresh herbs; toss again. Taste and adjust seasonings, including salt, pepper, and vinegar.

- Leftover cooked grains make perfect breakfast porridge. Just simmer them in a little milk (or soy, coconut, or one of the nut milks) and serve with fresh or dried fruits and nuts.

HEARTY GRAIN AND LEGUME SALAD

Serves 4 to 6

---

4 cups **Cooked Grains and/or Legumes** (page 101)

3 cups prepared **Vegetables** (page 103)

1 or 2 prepared **Flavorings** (page 106), ½ cup each

½ cup sliced **Onion** (page 106)

1 cup **Dressing** (pages 106 to 107)

---

1. Place the **Cooked Grains and/or Legumes** in a large bowl, along with the **Vegetables, Flavorings,** and **Onion.** (The salad ingredients and the dressing can be covered and refrigerated separately overnight. Keep salad ingredients segregated in the bowl until ready to dress.)

2. When ready to serve, add the **Dressing** to the salad ingredients and toss to coat. (Leftovers can be refrigerated for a couple of days.)

Black Bean and Corn (or Hominy) Salad with Cilantro-Lime Dressing

Stir in ½ a teaspoon ground cumin to the salad, if you like.

Grains and/or Legumes: black beans and corn (or hominy)
Vegetables: radishes and bell peppers
Flavorings: ¼ cup chopped pickled jalapeños and ½ cup pumpkin or sunflower seeds
Onion: red onion or scallions
Dressing: Herb Dressing (page 107) made with cilantro and lime juice

Lemony Lima Bean and Rice Salad with Asparagus and Fennel

Grains and/or Legumes: white rice and lima beans
Vegetables: asparagus and fennel
Flavorings: grated or shaved Parmesan cheese and chopped green olives
Onion: scallions
Dressing: Herb Dressing (page 107) made with parsley and lemon juice

Bulgur Wheat and White Bean Salad with Cucumber, Tomato, and Feta

Grains and/or Legumes: bulgur wheat and white beans
Vegetables: grape or cherry tomatoes and cucumber, lightly salted
Flavorings: chopped Kalamata olives and crumbled feta cheese
Onion: red onion
Dressing: Herb Dressing (page 107) made with parsley and red wine vinegar. Add fresh mint to the dressing, if you like.

Lentil and Brown Rice Salad with Brussels Sprouts, Walnuts, and Cranberries

Grains and/or Legumes: lentils and brown rice
Vegetables: carrots and Brussels sprouts
Flavorings: coarsely chopped toasted walnuts and dried cranberries
Onion: red onion or Pickled Pink Onions (page 53)
Dressing: Herb Dressing (page 107) made with parsley and balsamic vinegar

Asian-Flavored Rice and Green Pea Salad with Bean Sprouts and Peppers

Grains and/or Legumes: white rice and thawed frozen green peas
Vegetables: bell peppers and bean sprouts
Flavorings: ½ cup chopped roasted peanuts
Onion: scallions
Dressing: Asian Dressing (page 107)

Orecchiette and White Bean Salad with Cauliflower, Mushrooms, and Olives

Grains and/or Legumes: orecchiette pasta and cannellini beans
Vegetables: cauliflower and mushrooms
Flavorings: ½ cup pimiento-stuffed olives
Onion: red onion or Pickled Pink Onions (page 53)
Dressing: Herb Dressing (page 107) made with basil and red wine vinegar

Creamy Lentil and Barley Salad with Broccoli, Carrots, and Raisins

Brown rice in place of the barley is equally good here.

Grains and/or Legumes: lentils and barley
Vegetables: broccoli and carrots
Flavorings: raisins and sunflower seeds
Onion: red onion or Pickled Pink Onions (page 53)
Dressing: Creamy Herb Dressing (page 107) made with parsley

Couscous and Chickpea Salad with Peppers, Zucchini, Apricots, and Almonds

Grains and/or Legumes: couscous (Israeli or regular) and chickpeas
Vegetables: zucchini and red bell pepper
Flavorings: dates and toasted walnuts chopped
Onion: scallions
Dressing: Herb Dressing (page 107) made with balsamic vinegar, cilantro, and mint

---

At a Glance
HEARTY GRAIN AND LEGUME SALAD

1. Internalize the formula: 4 cups cooked legumes and/or grains, 3 cups vegetables, ½ to 1 cup flavorings, ½ cup onion, and 1 cup dressing.

2. Know the technique: Place all ingredients except dressing in a large bowl.

3. Add the dressing and toss to coat. Adjust seasonings and serve.

A Vat of Simple Tomato Sauce— So Many Different Meals

Pour a can of crushed tomatoes into a pan with a few
sizzling garlic cloves and you've got enough sauce
for a quick supper, but start with four cans instead of one
(with just a few more minutes of cooking time) and
you can quadruple the sauce for a head start on two other
meals later in the week.

Tomato Sauce Formula

A big pot of tomato sauce creates a range of meal possibilities. Siphon off a quart of sauce and simmer it with cauliflower and capers for a satisfying meatless spaghetti dinner. Add a can of evaporated milk and a pinch of nutmeg and baking soda to the second quart of sauce for an almost instant homemade cream of tomato soup: With bread, cheese, and fruit, it makes an easy appealing second meal. Transform the third quart of sauce into a quick chili: Just add it to sautéed onions, peppers, chili powder, and ground meat along with a couple of cans of pinto beans.

If you served spaghetti and tomato sauce three nights in a row, you might get some groans, but as everyone savors pasta one night, soup the next, and a Southwestern classic the following evening, they'll never suspect the same quick tomato sauce is at the heart of all three very different meals.

This is why you never make just one batch of tomato sauce!

TIPS AND TRICKS

- If using whole tomatoes packed in puree (San Marzano is my favorite), pour them into a big bowl and use your hands to crush them before adding them to the pot.

- Some brands of tomatoes are more acidic than others. Taste your sauce and if it's too tart, add up to 3 tablespoons sugar to balance or 1 teaspoon baking soda to neutralize some of the acidity in a four-can recipe. With both the sugar and baking soda, start by adding a little, then taste, and add more only as needed.

- Tomato brands also vary in thickness. If after 15 minutes of simmering, your sauce is not thick enough to mound slightly on a spoon, stir in enough tomato paste to achieve desired thickness.

A VAT OF SIMPLE TOMATO SAUCE, GARLICKY OR VEGETABLE

Makes more or less 3 quarts or enough for 3 meals (serving 4)

Whether you flavor the tomatoes with garlic or with celery, carrots, and onions, this sauce will become a kitchen staple. It's certainly true for me. There are many nights when I open the fridge wondering what to cook, and I sigh with relief when I spy a quart of this sauce.

Since I'm often in a hurry and mincing 12 garlic cloves is a lot, I buy peeled garlic cloves and mince them in the food processor, or I use the tubed garlic paste you find in the refrigerated section of the produce department. Figure ¼ cup of the garlic paste for the 12 cloves. Also, if there are kids in the house who don't like spicy, you may want to reduce the pepper flakes to ½ teaspoon or just omit it.

½ cup olive oil

12 large garlic cloves, minced, *or* 2 medium-large onions, 2 carrots, and 2 celery stalks, cut into small dice

1 teaspoon red pepper flakes

4 cans (28 ounces each) crushed tomatoes or whole tomatoes packed in puree (not juice!)

1 cup red or white wine or water

Salt and ground black pepper

1 can (6 ounces) tomato paste (if necessary; see Note)

1. **FOR GARLICKY TOMATO SAUCE (A):** Heat the oil, garlic, and pepper flakes in a large pot over medium-high heat until the garlic starts to sizzle, just a couple of minutes.

   FOR VEGETABLE TOMATO SAUCE (B): Heat the oil in a large pot over medium-high heat. Add the onions, carrots, celery, and pepper flakes and cook until vegetables soften, 5 to 7 minutes.

2. Stir in the tomatoes. Use the wine or water to rinse out the cans and add to the pot. Bring to a simmer, then reduce the heat to medium-low and simmer, partially covered, until the sauce thickens and the flavors meld, about 15 minutes. Taste the sauce and season with salt and pepper to taste. Add enough tomato paste so that you've made a thick, full-bodied sauce, not soup (see Note). Simmer to blend the flavors, a few minutes longer. Cool the sauce and divide it among 3 sealed containers. (Can be refrigerated for a couple of weeks or frozen for several months.)

Note: If using canned crushed tomatoes, you may not need any tomato paste. If using San Marzano whole tomatoes packed in puree (see Tips and Tricks, page 115), you will likely use the whole can of paste.

Suggestions

On a busy night, you can take one of the quarts of Simple Tomato Sauce (page 117) and use it as a base to build an interesting sauce to serve over pasta, a surprising stew to ladle over rice, or a comforting soup made complete with a warm baguette.

SAUCES TO SERVE OVER PASTA

Cook up some pasta, gnocchi, or ravioli. Once you've drained the cooked pasta, return it to the pot, toss it with one-third of the sauce, and divide among 4 pasta plates. Top each with a portion of the remaining sauce, a sprinkling of Parmesan cheese (preferably Parmigiano-Reggiano), and a little drizzle of extra-virgin olive oil. Each generous quart container of sauce is enough for 12 to 16 ounces of pasta—enough to serve 4 or 5 people. You can also flavor it with one or more of the following to change it up or make it more interesting. Here are some suggested ingredients to add to one of the quarts. Cook these sauces in a large saucepan or small pot.

CREAMY TOMATO SAUCE WITH PROSCIUTTO AND CHICKPEAS

If you want to make this vegetarian, simply omit the prosciutto. Additionally, to make it vegan, substitute coconut creamer for the heavy cream.

Cook: 2 ounces (4 thin slices) thin-sliced prosciutto, minced, in a couple of teaspoons olive oil in a large saucepan or small pot over medium-high heat until soft, about 2 minutes.

Add: 1 quart Simple Tomato Sauce, Garlicky or Vegetable (page 117); 1 can chickpeas (15 to 16 ounces), drained and coarsely chopped; 1 teaspoon dried basil, and ¼ cup heavy cream. Bring to a simmer, then simmer 5 minutes to blend the flavors. Adjust the seasonings and serve.

QUICK CACCIATORE

Cook: 1 thinly sliced onion and ½ bell pepper, cut into short strips, in a generous tablespoon olive oil in a large saucepan or small pot over medium-high heat, seasoning with salt and pepper, until soft, about 5 minutes.

Add: 1 quart Garlicky Tomato Sauce (page 117), 8 ounces (a heaping 2 cups) shredded cooked chicken, ½ teaspoon dried basil, and ¼ teaspoon dried oregano. Bring to a simmer, then simmer 5 minutes to blend the flavors. Adjust the seasonings and serve.

TOMATO SAUCE WITH CAULIFLOWER AND CAPERS

Cook: 2 cups small cauliflower florets in 1 tablespoon oil in a large saucepan or small pot over medium-high heat, seasoning with salt and pepper, until golden, about 5 minutes.

Add: 1 quart Garlicky Tomato Sauce (page 117), ½ teaspoon dried oregano, and 2 tablespoons drained capers. Bring to a simmer and continue to simmer until the cauliflower is tender, 5 to 7 minutes. Adjust the seasonings and serve.

TOMATO SAUCE WITH TUNA AND OLIVES

Simmer: 1 quart Garlicky Tomato Sauce (page 117) in a large saucepan or small pot.

Add: 2 undrained cans (7 ounces each) water-packed tuna and ½ cup coarsely chopped pitted Kalamata olives. Simmer 5 minutes to blend the flavors. Adjust the seasonings and serve.

PUTTANESCA SAUCE

Simmer: 1 quart Garlicky Tomato Sauce (page 117) in a large saucepan or small pot.

Add: 4 minced anchovy fillets, ½ cup coarsely chopped pitted dry-cured olives, and 2 tablespoons drained capers. Simmer 5 minutes to blend the flavors. Adjust the seasonings and serve.

TOMATO SAUCE WITH MUSHROOMS, BACON, AND THYME

Cook: 4 ounces (3 thick slices) bacon, diced, in a large saucepan or small pot over medium-high heat, until most of the fat has rendered, about 5 minutes. Drain all but 1 tablespoon of the drippings.

Add and cook: ½ pound sliced baby bella mushrooms, seasoning with salt and pepper, until browned, about 5 minutes. Add 1 teaspoon dried thyme and 1 quart Simple Tomato Sauce, Garlicky or Vegetable (page 117). Simmer 5 minutes to blend the flavors. Adjust the seasonings and serve.

FRA DIAVOLO SAUCE

The tomato sauce already has a subtle kick, but if you want a little more heat, add another pinch of red pepper flakes.

Simmer: 1 quart Garlicky Tomato Sauce (page 117) in a large saucepan or small pot.

Add: 1 pound peeled shrimp cut into bite-size pieces and 2 tablespoons chopped fresh parsley. Simmer until the shrimp turn pink, a couple of minutes longer. Adjust the seasonings and serve.

GREEK-STYLE TOMATO SAUCE

Instead of grated Parmesan, sprinkle the dish with a little crumbled feta.

Cook: 1 pound ground lamb (or beef) in a large saucepan or small pot over medium-high heat until it loses its raw color. Spoon off the excess fat.

Add: 2 teaspoons ground cinnamon, 1 teaspoon dried oregano, 1 quart Garlicky Tomato Sauce (page 117), and ⅓ cup raisins. Bring to a simmer and simmer 5 minutes to blend the flavors and soften the raisins. Adjust the seasonings and serve.

QUICK BOLOGNESE

You can use ground beef or bulk Italian sausage in place of the meatloaf mix.

Cook: 2 ounces (4 thin slices) prosciutto, minced, in a couple of teaspoons olive oil in large saucepan or small pot over medium-high heat until they turn brown, a couple of minutes.

Add: 1 pound meatloaf mix (a mix of pork, veal, and beef). Cook until it loses its raw color, then spoon off excess fat. Add a generous quart Vegetable Tomato Sauce (page 117) and simmer until the sauce thickens, about 10 minutes.

Stir in: ¼ cup heavy cream and simmer a couple of minutes longer. Adjust the seasonings and serve.

TOMATO SAUCE WITH BACON, BAY SCALLOPS, AND BASIL

Cook: 4 ounces (3 thick slices) bacon, diced, in a large saucepan or small pot over medium-high heat until most of the fat has rendered, about 5 minutes. Drain off the fat. Add 1 quart Garlicky Tomato Sauce (page 117) and bring to a simmer.

Add: 1 pound scallops (if frozen, thaw and drain) that have been sprinkled with salt and ¼ cup chopped fresh basil leaves. Cook until scallops are just opaque, a couple of minutes. Adjust the seasonings and serve.

RED CLAM SAUCE

If you happen to have fresh parsley in the fridge, add a couple of tablespoons along with the clams.

Simmer: 1 quart Garlicky Tomato Sauce (page 117), the juices drained from 2 cans (10 ounces each) whole baby clams (reserve clams), 1 teaspoon dried basil, and ½ teaspoon dried oregano in a small saucepan or large pot until sauce has reduced to original thickness, about 10 minutes.

Add: reserved clams and heat through. Adjust the seasonings and serve.

TOMATO SAUCE WITH SAUSAGE AND PEPPERS

Cook: 1 pound bulk Italian sausage in a large saucepan or small pot over medium-high heat until it loses its raw color and spoon off any excess fat.

Add: 1 halved and thinly sliced medium onion and 1 small bell pepper, cut into short, thin strips. Cook until softened, about 5 minutes. Add 1 quart Garlicky Tomato Sauce (page 117) and simmer 5 minutes to blend the flavors. Adjust the seasonings and serve.

VODKA SAUCE

Simmer: 1 quart Garlicky Tomato Sauce (page 117) with ½ cup heavy cream in a large saucepan or small pot to reduce slightly and blend the flavors, about 5 minutes.

Stir in: 3 tablespoons vodka and serve.

CUSTOMIZE YOUR OWN (CYO) SAUCE

Create your own sauce with what you have around. Stir in 1 or more of the following ingredients to create your own Italian-style sauce to serve with pasta:

MEATY AND VEGETARIAN (CHOOSE 1, OPTIONAL)

- 1 pound peeled raw shrimp, cut into bite-size pieces
- 1 pound raw bay scallops, drained
- 1 pound fully cooked sausages (your choice), cut into a medium dice
- 2 cups (about 10 ounces), shredded rotisserie chicken, light or dark meat
- 2 cans (7ounces each) tuna, undrained
- 4 cans (6.5 ounces each) chopped clams or 2 10-ounce whole baby clams, drained
- 2 cups cooked drained white beans, such as cannellini, navy, or Great Northern
- 2 cups diced roasted (page 39) or grilled vegetables (page 43)

FLAVORINGS (CHOOSE 1 OR 2)

- **Kalamata or pimiento-stuffed olives:** ⅓ cup chopped
- **Capers:** 2 tablespoons drained
- **Caramelized Onions (page 51):** ⅓ cup
- **Roasted red peppers:** ⅓ cup chopped
- **Pesto:** ¼ cup
- **Basil:** ¼ cup chopped fresh or 1 teaspoon dried
- **Parsley:** ¼ cup chopped fresh leaves
- **Oregano, dried:** ½ teaspoon
- **Thyme leaves, dried:** ½ teaspoon

SAUCES TO SERVE OVER RICE

When you realize that tomato sauce is really just cooked tomatoes, oil, and aromatics, you start to see it can be used as a base for dishes far beyond Italian-inspired. Having a quart of cooked tomato sauce not only gives you a head start on the ingredient prep, but also reduces cooking time since you're starting with a rich, reduced base. Change the spice profile, add a few different ingredients, and sub in rice for the pasta and you've got a completely different meal from the one the night before. Serve any of the following sauces with ¾ to 1 cup of cooked rice per person (see page 61 for cooking instructions for both white and brown rice).

SAUSAGE CREOLE

This Creole sauce can easily be transformed with a switch in protein. Using 1 pound cubed boneless, skinless chicken thighs instead of sausages makes it Chicken Creole. For Shrimp Creole, omit the sausages and stir in 1 pound peeled shrimp, cut into bite-size pieces, during the last few minutes of cooking. Of course, a combo is always good—especially half of each: sausage and shrimp.

Cook: 1 pound sliced smoked sausage, such as kielbasa, in 1 tablespoon oil in a large pot over medium-high heat until browned, 4 to 5 minutes. Add and sauté ½ large bell pepper, cut into short strips, until softened, 1 to 2 minutes longer.

Add: 1 quart Vegetable Tomato Sauce (page 117), 1 cup water, and 1 tablespoon Creole seasoning and bring to a simmer. Reduce the heat to medium-low and simmer 10 minutes to blend the flavors. Adjust the seasonings and serve.

COUNTRY CAPTAIN

Popular both in the US and in Mumbai, this curried chicken stew, flavored with onion, peppers, tomatoes, curry, and raisins, is one of the earliest Anglo-Indian fusion dishes.

Cook: the skinned side of 6 large boneless, skinless chicken thighs that have been oiled, salted, peppered, and sprinkled with 2 teaspoons curry powder in large pot over medium-high heat until browned, about 5 minutes.

Turn the chicken and add: 1 bell pepper, cut into short strips, and 3 garlic cloves, minced, and cook a minute or two longer. Add 1 quart Vegetable Tomato Sauce (page 117), 1 tablespoon curry powder, and ⅓ cup raisins or currants. Bring to a simmer and continue to simmer until the chicken has cooked through and the flavors have blended, about 10 minutes. Adjust the seasonings and serve.

CHICKEN TIKKA MASALA

The tubed ginger paste that you find in the refrigerated section of many produce departments is a good shortcut here.

Cook: the skinned side of 6 large boneless, skinless chicken thighs that have been oiled, salted, peppered, and sprinkled with 1½ teaspoons ground coriander, and 1½ teaspoons ground cumin in a large pot over medium-high heat until browned, about 5 minutes.

Turn the chicken and add: 1 diced medium onion and 2 tablespoons grated fresh ginger and cook a minute or two longer. Add 2 tablespoons garam masala, 1 quart Garlicky Tomato Sauce (page 117), and 1 can (13.5 ounces) coconut milk. Bring to a simmer and continue to simmer for 10 minutes to blend the flavors. Adjust the seasonings, stir in ¼ cup chopped fresh cilantro, and serve.

AFRICAN CHICKEN STEW WITH SWEET POTATOES AND COLLARDS

Cook: the skinned side of 6 large boneless, skinless chicken thighs that have been oiled, salted, and peppered in a large pot over medium-high heat, until browned, about 5 minutes.

Turn the chicken and add: 2 tablespoons grated fresh ginger and 2 tablespoons minced garlic (or refrigerated pastes) and cook a minute or so longer. Add 1 quart of Vegetable Tomato Sauce (page 117), 1 quart chicken broth, and 2 diced sweet potatoes. Bring to a simmer and continue to simmer until potatoes are almost tender, about 10 minutes. Stir in 1 pound chopped collards and 6 tablespoons peanut butter and continue to cook until the collards wilt, a couple of minutes longer. Adjust the seasonings, stirring in ¼ cup chopped fresh cilantro, and serve.

SAUCE BECOMES SOUP

There's a whole world of tomato-based soups besides the obvious cream of tomato, so consider using one of your quarts of sauce to make a quick pot for lunch or dinner.

CLASSIC CREAM OF TOMATO SOUP

Simmer: 1 quart Simple Tomato Sauce, Garlicky or Vegetable (page 117), in a large pot.

Add: ¼ teaspoon baking soda, stirring until the bubbling subsides, followed by 1 can (12 ounces) evaporated milk and ¼ teaspoon ground nutmeg. Simmer to heat through. Adjust the seasonings and serve.

WEEKNIGHT CHILI

Cook: 1 chopped onion and ½ chopped bell pepper in 1 tablespoon oil in a large pot over medium-high heat until tender, about 5 minutes.

Add: 1 pound ground beef or turkey, ¼ cup chili powder, and 1 teaspoon dried oregano and cook until the meat loses its raw color. Add 1 generous quart Garlicky Tomato Sauce (page 117) and 1 can (15 to 16 ounces) pinto beans, drained, and simmer 10 minutes to blend the flavors. Stir in ½ ounce bitter or semisweet chocolate and serve.

MANHATTAN CLAM CHOWDER

Cook: 2 ounces (4 thin slices) prosciutto, minced, in a couple of teaspoons olive oil in a large pot over medium-high heat until browned, a couple of minutes.

Add: 1 quart Vegetable Tomato Sauce (page 117), 2 cups cubed potatoes, the juice drained from 3 cans (6 ounces each) minced clams (reserve clams), 1 bottle (8 ounces) clam juice, and ½ teaspoon dried thyme leaves. Bring to a simmer and continue to simmer until the potatoes are tender, about 10 minutes. Stir in minced clams, and serve.

TOMATO SOUP WITH HAM, CABBAGE, AND WHITE BEANS

Cook: ½ pound ham, diced in 1 tablespoon olive oil in a large pot over medium-high heat to intensify flavor, a couple of minutes. Add 1 medium diced onion and cook until softened, a few minutes longer.

Add: 1 quart Garlicky Tomato Sauce (page 117), 1 quart chicken broth, 2 cans (15 to 16 ounces each) white beans, drained, ½ pound shredded cabbage (scant 3 cups), and 2 teaspoons Italian seasoning. Bring to a simmer and continue to simmer 10 minutes to blend the flavors. Serve.

PASTA E FAGIOLI

This calls for Vegetable Tomato Sauce, but if you only have Garlicky Tomato Sauce on hand, simply sauté 1 each: chopped celery, carrot, and onion after frying the prosciutto, and omit the extra 3 garlic cloves below.

Cook: 2 ounces (4 thin slices) prosciutto, minced, in a couple teaspoons of oil in a large pot over medium-high heat until browned, a couple of minutes. Add 3 garlic cloves, minced, and fry until fragrant.

Add: 1 quart Vegetable Tomato Sauce (page 117), 1 quart chicken broth, 2 cans (15 to 16 ounces each) cannellini beans, drained, and 1 tablespoon minced fresh rosemary. Bring to a simmer and add 1½ cups small pasta shape, such as ditalini or small shells, and continue to simmer until tender, about 10 minutes. Serve.

MINESTRONE SOUP

If you want to add a little pasta to the soup, use only 1 can beans and add ¾ cup small pasta, such as ditalini or small shells. Or, to make it vegetarian, omit the sausage and sauté the diced bell pepper in 1 tablespoon oil. Use vegetable broth instead of chicken broth.

Cook: ½ pound bulk Italian sausage in a large pot over medium-high heat until it loses its raw color. Add 1 diced bell pepper and cook until softened, just a few minutes.

Add: 2 cups diced zucchini, 2 cups fresh or frozen green beans, 1 quart Vegetable Tomato Sauce (page 117), 1 quart chicken broth, 2 cans (15 to 16 ounces each) kidney beans, drained, and 2 teaspoons Italian seasoning. Bring to a simmer and continue to simmer 10 minutes to blend the flavors. Add 2 cups packed chopped kale and 1 cup frozen peas during the last few minutes. Serve.

At a Glance
A VAT OF TOMATO SAUCE

1. Internalize the formula: ½ cup olive oil; 12 garlic cloves or 2 each celery stalks, carrots, and onions, diced; 1 teaspoon red pepper flakes; 4 cans (28 ounces each) tomatoes; 1 cup wine, and tomato paste if needed.

2. Know the technique: Heat garlic and pepper flakes in oil (or sauté celery, carrots, and onions in oil with pepper flakes). Add tomatoes and wine. Simmer to thick sauce consistency. Add tomato paste to thicken, if necessary. Adjust the seasonings.

3. Use as is or follow one of the suggestions on pages 118 to 121 using 1 quart sauce. Divide the remaining sauce into two containers and refrigerate or freeze.

TOMATO SAUCE

Chicken Tikka Masala

Weeknight Chili

Pasta with Vegetables

Dinner is a good place to get your daily dose of vegetables, so pasta with vegetables and a salad is a regular on our menu. Zucchini is an easier sell— especially with kids—when tossed with ziti.

Start by pulling out a pot and a skillet, then open the fridge and take inventory of your vegetable supply, and move to the pantry to choose your pasta. If you happen to have a few eggs, a container of ricotta, a jar of pesto, or a cup of Simple Tomato Sauce (page 117) or good quality store-bought marinara, even better. Now you've got the start for a healthy supper for just about any night, but especially Meatless Mondays!

Pasta with Vegetables Formula: Firm, Leafy, and Tender

For this chapter, I start with a general formula for Pasta with Vegetables that explains the basic ratios. I then show you how to apply that formula to three different categories of vegetables: firm, tender, and leafy—the most essential difference among them is how the vegetables are cooked.

PASTA: 12 Ounces

I used to call for a pound of pasta for four people, but over the years I've moved those ounces from the pasta to the vegetable column. Better to eat more vegetables than pasta! You may want to cook a whole pound of pasta so there are leftovers, but you don't need to cook a full pound for four people.

Take note of the pasta cooking water amount. As long as you stir the pasta at the beginning to keep it from sticking, you can save precious time by cooking the pasta in 2 quarts water rather than the full gallon most recipes call for. The boiling pasta (which is just flour, after all) releases body and flavor into the relatively small amount of water, good for moistening the cooked pasta dish.

You can cheat the water, but not the salt. For well-seasoned pasta you need a generously salted pot of water. Figure a generous tablespoon of table salt for 2 quarts water. Short stubby pastas, such as penne, fusilli, and bow ties, are ideal for this technique. Angel hair needs a moister sauce, so only use it if you plan to stir in one of the enrichments like ricotta, tomato sauce, pesto, or eggs.

VEGETABLES: 1 Pound (or a Little More)

A generous pound of prepared vegetables is ideal for Pasta with Vegetables, so buy a little extra so there's still a pound after peeling, seeding, stemming, coring, and/or trimming.

To make Pasta with Vegetables, first understand that there are three kinds of vegetables—firm, tender, and leafy, each one needing a particular cooking method.

FIRM VEGETABLES like broccoli, cauliflower, asparagus, cabbage, snow peas, sugar snaps, carrots, and potatoes need moist heat to soften them and then a little direct heat to bring out their flavor, so those get steam-sautéed (see more on this method on page 47).

TENDER VEGETABLES like bell peppers, onions, mushrooms, leeks, eggplant, zucchini, yellow squash, and fennel are high-moisture and need the high, dry heat of the sauté pan to evaporate that moisture and intensify flavor.

LEAFY GREENS, both tender (spinach, Swiss chard, and beet greens) and sturdy (turnip, mustard, collard, kale, and broccoli rabe) cook with the pasta, resulting in a flavorful liquid, some of which gets reserved to toss with the pasta.

FAT: 4 Tablespoons

Without fat, pasta with vegetables would be boring, dry, and lifeless. Fat adds body, flavor, and mouthfeel. Which fat should you use? Fat is fat, so feel free to use them interchangeably here. Keep in mind that butter and bacon drippings offer great flavor, but if cholesterol is a problem, opt for olive oil. If you like bacon in your pasta but want to avoid the saturated fat, drain off the drippings and replace it with olive oil. You can also split the fat and use half bacon drippings or butter and half olive oil.

AROMATICS: Onion or Garlic

Fat contributes to flavor, and so do onion and garlic. Like the fats in this formula, these two aromatic vegetables are interchangeable. And there's nothing stopping you from adding them both, if you like.

FLAVORINGS

What you've got in your pantry will determine how you flavor your pasta. If it's winter, dried herbs are a likely choice. If it's summer and your herb box is abundant, fresh herbs always enliven a pasta dish. As with most of the other formulas, dried herbs are cooked with the dish, fresh herbs are added at the end when tossing the pasta. The only exceptions are woody fresh herbs like thyme and rosemary, which should be treated like dried.

In addition to herbs, you can add Italian-inspired flavorings like olives, nuts, prosciutto, finely grated lemon zest, or a little pinch of pepper flakes to stimulate the tongue. Fresh flavorings like lemon zest are added at the end with the fresh herbs. Add other flavorings when instructed. You can also bulk up and flavor any Pasta with Vegetables by stirring in a can (15 to 16 ounces) of drained white beans to the skillet when instructed to add optional flavorings and/ or dried herbs.

ENRICHMENTS

The best way I know to add flavor and moisture to Pasta with Vegetables is to stir in one of the following when tossing the pasta:

- 1 cup ricotta cheese, part-skim or whole milk
- 1 cup Simple Tomato Sauce, Garlicky or Vegetable (page 117), or good-quality jarred marinara, warmed
- ¼ cup pesto
- 4 large eggs, whisked

TIPS AND TRICKS

- If you've got roasted vegetables around (see A Pan of Roasted Vegetables, page 39), follow the technique for Pasta with Firm Vegetables (page 133), sautéing garlic and flavorings of your choice. Then, when tossing the pasta, add 2 cups warm roasted vegetables for a nearly effortless supper.
- To keep pasta water from boiling over, use a large—at least 8-quart—pot, and only partially cover the pasta during cooking.
- Explore other grain- and legume-based pastas, such as chickpea and lentil.
- Once you've mastered the techniques, you can mix vegetables from the different categories. Make pasta with bell peppers (from the tender vegetable category) and spinach (from the greens category). Try a mix of half each leeks and asparagus, or kale and butternut squash.

Pasta with Firm Vegetables

Firm vegetables need a little moist heat before they sauté. You can accomplish this seamlessly in one skillet by cooking the vegetable in a small amount of water, salt, and fat. Steaming it over high heat causes the water to evaporate quickly, at which point the fat kicks in and the vegetable starts to sauté. Cooking this way is quick and efficient, and you retain the vegetable's flavor.

FIRM VEGETABLES: Generous 1 Pound

The following firm vegetables are the most obvious candidates for pasta dishes.

- **Asparagus:** Snap off tough ends and cut into 1-inch lengths (thinly slice thick asparagus spears lengthwise).
- **Broccoli crowns or cauliflower:** Cut into small florets. (Peel and thinly slice any broccoli stems.) Or, buy packaged florets.
- **Brussels sprouts:** Trim root end and halve lengthwise.
- **Turnips, rutabagas, or winter squash, such as butternut:** Peel and cut into bite-size chunks (seed winter squash).
- **Cabbage:** Halve, core, and thinly slice.
- **Carrots:** Peel and cut (on the diagonal, if you like) into slices ¼ inch thick.
- **Green beans, thin or haricots verts:** Trim ends and snap into bite-size pieces.
- **New or red potatoes:** Quarter if small, or cut into bite-size chunks if large.
- **Snow peas or sugar snap peas:** Stem (and string, if necessary) and halve crosswise.

PASTA WITH FIRM VEGETABLES

Serves 4

Table salt

12 ounces dried pasta

4 tablespoons **Fat** (olive oil, butter, or fat rendered from sausage or bacon, see Note)

Aromatic: 3 garlic cloves, minced, or 1 medium-large onion, halved and thinly sliced

1 to 1¼ pounds prepared **Firm Vegetables** (see page 129)

Flavorings (see Note)

Enrichments (optional; see page 131)

½ cup grated Parmesan cheese, plus more for serving

Ground black pepper

---

1. Bring 2 quarts water and 1 tablespoon salt to a boil in a large pot over medium-high heat. Using the back-of-the-box cooking times as a guide, cook the pasta, partially covered and stirring frequently, until the pasta is al dente.

2. Meanwhile, bring ⅓ cup water, ½ teaspoon salt, the **Fat, Aromatic, Firm Vegetables,** and any **Flavorings** (except fresh ones) to full steam in a large covered skillet. (Steam will start to seep out between the lid and skillet.) Continue to steam over high heat until the vegetables are brightly colored and just tender, 5 to 7 minutes, depending on their size. Uncover and continue to cook until the liquid evaporates and the vegetables start to sauté and turn golden brown, 1 to 2 minutes longer. If using pork, return it to the skillet now.

3. Reserving 1 cup of the pasta cooking liquid, drain the pasta. Return the pasta to the pot, add the contents of the skillet, some of the pasta cooking liquid, any fresh **Flavorings** and/or optional **Enrichments,** and the Parmesan, tossing to coat. Add more water if needed. Taste and adjust the seasonings, including salt and pepper. Serve with additional cheese passed separately.

Note about Flavorings: This can be dried herbs, spices, or flavorings like olives, which cook with the vegetables. Fresh flavorings like herbs and zests are added at the end when tossing the Parmesan cheese with the pasta. See page 130 for ideas and general guidelines.

Note about pork rendering: If using pork rendering as the fat, first cook the bacon or sausage in a large skillet over medium-high heat until cooked. Remove the pork with a slotted spoon and set aside. Eyeballing the amount, drain the rendering or add more oil to equal 4 tablespoons. Using the same skillet, proceed with step 2.

Pasta with Asparagus, Lemon, and Parsley

If you like, add ½ cup frozen green peas to the cooked pasta shortly before draining it.

Vegetables: asparagus
Fat: butter
Aromatic: onion
Flavorings: 1 teaspoon finely grated lemon zest
Enrichment: ¼ cup pesto

Quick Pasta Primavera

Frozen peas are good in this pasta, too—add ½ cup to the cooking pasta shortly before draining it.

Vegetables: asparagus, carrots, and sugar snap peas
Fat: butter
Aromatic: onion
Flavorings: ¼ cup chopped fresh parsley leaves and 2 tablespoons snipped fresh chives or scallion greens
Enrichment: 1 cup ricotta cheese

Pasta with Brussels Sprouts, Butternut Squash, Bacon, and Thyme

If you don't like one of the vegetables, make it with all Brussels sprouts or all butternut squash. This dish would be equally good with sausage.

Vegetables: butternut squash and Brussels sprouts
Fat: ¼ cup rendered bacon fat from 4 slices thick-cut bacon, cut into ½-inch pieces
Aromatic: garlic
Flavorings: ½ teaspoon dried thyme leaves
Enrichment: none

Pasta with Cauliflower (or Green Beans), Tomatoes, and Olives

Vegetables: cauliflower or green beans
Fat: olive oil
Aromatic: garlic
Flavorings: ½ cup chopped Kalamata olives, ¼ cup chopped fresh parsley
Enrichment: 1 cup warm Simple Tomato Sauce (page 117) or good-quality jarred marinara

Pasta with Broccoli, Garlic, and Red Pepper Flakes

If you've got Prosciutto Crisps (page 64) in your larder, sprinkle them on, along with a little Parmesan cheese. They only take a few minutes to make, so if you've got time, cook up a few slices while the pasta boils.

Vegetables: broccoli
Fat: olive oil
Aromatic: garlic
Flavorings: ½ teaspoon red pepper flakes and/or ½ teaspoon herbes de Provence.
Enrichment: 1 cup warm Simple Tomato Sauce (page 117) or good-quality jarred marinara

Pasta with Cabbage, Potatoes, Bacon, and Thyme

Stir the eggs quickly into the hot pasta so that they thicken without curdling.

Fat: ¼ cup rendered fat from 4 slices thick-cut bacon, cut into ½-inch pieces
Aromatic: garlic or onion
Vegetables: cabbage and potatoes
Flavorings: ½ teaspoon dried thyme leaves or caraway seeds
Enrichment: 4 beaten eggs

At a Glance

PASTA WITH FIRM VEGETABLES

1. Internalize the formula: 12 ounces pasta, a generous 1 pound vegetables, 4 tablespoons fat, garlic or onion, flavorings, and optional enrichments—and don't forget the Parmesan cheese!

2. Know the technique: Cook the pasta. Reserving 1 cup of the cooking water; return the pasta to the pot.

3. Steam the vegetables until tender in a covered skillet with ⅓ cup water, salt, fat, garlic and/or onion, and flavorings (except fresh ones).

4. Uncover and continue to cook until the liquid evaporates and the vegetables start to sauté and turn golden brown.

5. Toss the drained pasta, the contents of the skillet, the Parmesan cheese, fresh flavorings and/or enrichments (if using), and enough cooking liquid to moisten. Adjust the seasonings.

Pasta *with* Leafy Greens,
Tomatoes, White Beans,
and Olives

Pasta *with* **Mushrooms, Rosemary,** *and* **Garlic**

Pasta *with* **Bell Peppers, Capers,** *and* **Basil**

Pasta *with* **Brussels Sprouts, Butternut Squash, Bacon,** *and* **Thyme**

Pasta with Leafy Greens

When served as a side dish, tender greens are typically sautéed and hardy greens are braised, but when cooking them for pasta, they all cook the same way: In the last few minutes of cooking, just drop the greens—tender or hardy—into the pasta pot and cook them all together. This method not only keeps the greens from clumping, but also results in a flavorful broth, some of which gets reserved and used to moisten and flavor the pasta dish.

LEAFY GREENS: Generous 1 Pound

These days, so many greens come cleaned, stemmed, cut, and bagged. If you purchase already prepared greens, 1 pound is enough. But if you choose to buy them by the bunch, you need to stem and trim the greens, so buy extra so that you end up with a pound of actual greens. Here's how to clean, stem, and cut them. The following greens are all perfect pasta partners:

- **Beet or turnip greens:** Hold each leaf between thumb and index finger of one hand while pulling back the center rib with the other. Wash and coarse-chop.
- **Bok choy:** Thinly slice crisp edible stems and coarse-chop leaves; wash.
- **Broccoli rabe:** Peel stems, if tough, then coarse-chop leaves and stems and wash.
- **Curly endive and escarole:** Trim the root end. Coarse-chop and wash the greens.
- **Kale, collards, mustard greens, or Swiss chard:** Slash down both sides of each leaf with a sharp knife. Wash and coarse-chop leaves.
- **Spinach:** For large mature spinach with tough stems, hold each leaf between thumb and index finger of one hand while pulling back the stem and central rib with the other; wash. For baby spinach, just make sure they're clean.

PASTA WITH LEAFY GREENS

Serves 4 to 6

---

1 pound prepared **Leafy Greens** (see page 140)

Table salt

12 ounces dried pasta

4 tablespoons **Fat** (olive oil, butter, or rendered pork fat from sausage or bacon, see Note)

Aromatic: 3 garlic cloves or 1 medium-large onion, halved and thinly sliced

Flavorings (see Note)

Enrichments (optional; see page 131)

½ cup grated Parmesan cheese, plus more for serving

Ground black pepper

---

1. Bring 2 quarts water and 1 tablespoon salt to a boil in a large pot over medium-high heat. Using the back-of-the-box cooking times as a guide, cook the pasta, partially covered and stirring frequently, until about 5 minutes away from being done. Add the **Leafy Greens** to the pot of partially cooked pasta; cook, stirring to wilt the greens, until the pasta is al dente and the greens are just tender, 5 to 7 minutes longer.

2. Meanwhile, if using garlic, heat the **Fat** and garlic in a medium skillet until the garlic starts to sizzle. If using onion, heat the **Fat** over medium-high heat, add the onion, and sauté until soft and golden. Add any **Flavorings** (except fresh ones) and sauté about 1 minute to blend the flavors. Set the skillet aside.

3. Reserving 1 cup of the cooking liquid, drain the pasta and return it to the pot. Add the contents of the skillet, some of the reserved cooking liquid, any optional fresh **Flavorings** and/or **Enrichments**, and the Parmesan, tossing to coat. Taste and adjust the seasonings, including pepper to taste. Serve with additional cheese passed separately.

Note on Flavorings: This can be dried herbs, spices, or flavorings like olives, which cook with the aromatic. Fresh flavorings like herbs and zests are added at the end when tossing the Parmesan cheese with the pasta. See page 130 for ideas and general guidelines.

Note about pork rendering: If using pork rendering as the fat, first cook the bacon or sausage in a medium skillet over medium-high heat until cooked. Remove the pork with a slotted spoon and set aside. Eyeballing the amount, drain the rendering or add more oil to equal 4 tablespoons. Using the same skillet, proceed with step 2.

Pasta with Leafy Greens, Prosciutto, Lemon, and Red Pepper Flakes

To keep this dish vegetarian, substitute ¼ cup pine nuts for the prosciutto, and sauté them until the nuts are fragrant and golden.

Vegetables: any prepared leafy green
Fat: olive oil
Aromatic: garlic
Flavorings: 2 ounces (4 thin slices) prosciutto, minced, ½ teaspoon red pepper flakes, and 1 teaspoon grated lemon zest
Enrichment: none

Follow the Pasta with Leafy Greens formula, adding prosciutto and pepper flakes when instructed to add the Flavorings in step 2, and add lemon zest when instructed to add fresh Flavorings in step 3.

Pasta with Leafy Greens, Tomatoes, White Beans, and Olives

Vegetables: any prepared leafy green
Fat: olive oil
Aromatic: garlic
Flavorings: 1 can (15 to 16 ounces) white beans, drained; ½ cup chopped Kalamata olives
Enrichment: 1 cup warm Simple Tomato Sauce (page 117) or good-quality jarred marinara

Follow the Pasta with Leafy Greens formula, adding the white beans and olives when instructed to add the Flavorings in step 2.

Pasta with Leafy Greens, Sausage, and Garlic

If you can only get sausage links, simply remove the sausage from the casing. If you don't want to use rendered sausage fat, drain it once the sausage has browned and replace it with olive oil.

Vegetables: any prepared leafy green
Fat: ¼ cup rendered sausage fat from ½ pound bulk spicy Italian sausages
Aromatic: garlic
Enrichment: none

Pasta with Leafy Greens, Bacon, and Red Pepper Flakes

Vegetables: any prepared leafy green
Fat: ¼ cup rendered bacon fat from 4 slices thick-cut bacon, cut into ½-inch pieces
Aromatic: garlic
Flavorings: ½ teaspoon red pepper flakes
Enrichment: none

At a Glance

PASTA WITH LEAFY GREENS

1. Internalize the formula: 12 ounces pasta, a generous 1 pound of greens, 4 tablespoons fat, aromatic (garlic or onion), flavorings, and optional enrichments—and don't forget the Parmesan cheese!

2. Know the technique: Add the greens to the boiling pasta when it is about 5 minutes away from done.

3. Reserving 1 cup of the cooking water, drain the pasta and greens and return to the pot.

4. If using garlic, add it to the heating fat until the garlic just starts to sizzle. If using onion, add it to the hot fat and sauté until softened.

5. Stir in flavorings (except fresh ones) into the softened garlic and/or onion. Cook to blend the flavors.

6. Toss the drained pasta, contents of the skillet, fresh flavorings and/or enrichments (if using), Parmesan cheese, and cooking liquid as needed. Adjust the seasonings.

Pasta with Tender Vegetables

Pasta tossed with tender vegetables—those that need direct high heat to evaporate moisture and intensify flavors—make great meatless dinners, too.

TENDER VEGETABLES: Generous 1 Pound

The following vegetables are some of the most ideal candidates for Pasta with Tender Vegetables:

- **Bell peppers of any color:** Stem, seed, and cut into thin, short strips.
- **Cabbage:** Halve, core, and thinly slice.
- **Eggplant:** Trim and cut into medium dice.
- **Fennel:** Trim and reserve fronds. Halve (or quarter, if large), core, and thinly slice.
- **Leeks:** Trim off the tough dark green tops and discard. Quarter lengthwise, then cut crosswise into ½-inch-thick slices. Wash in a bowl of cold water.
- **Mushrooms:** For white and baby bella mushrooms, trim stem ends, rinse if dirty, and slice. For larger portobello mushrooms, remove stems, halve or quarter and thinly slice.
- **Onions:** Peel, halve from root to stem end, and thinly slice crosswise.
- **Yellow squash or zucchini:** Trim ends and cut into medium dice.

PASTA WITH TENDER VEGETABLES

Serves 4 to 6

Table salt

12 ounces dried pasta

4 tablespoons **Fat** (olive oil, butter, or rendered pork fat from sausage or bacon, see Note)

Aromatics: 3 minced garlic cloves or 1 medium-large onion, halved and thinly sliced

1 to 1¼ pounds prepared **Tender Vegetables** (see page 129)

Ground black pepper

Flavorings (see Note)

Enrichments (optional, see page 131)

½ cup grated Parmesan cheese, plus more for serving

1. Bring 2 quarts water and 1 tablespoon salt to a boil in a large pot over medium-high heat. Using the back-of-the-box cooking times as a guide, cook the pasta, partially covered and stirring frequently, until the pasta is al dente.

2. Meanwhile, if using garlic, heat the **Fat** and garlic in a large skillet over medium-high heat until the garlic just starts to sizzle. If using onion, heat the **Fat** over medium-high heat. Add the onion and sauté until it has softened, 3 to 4 minutes. Add the **Tender Vegetables** to the pan, sprinkle generously with salt and pepper, and sauté until tender, 5 to 7 minutes longer. Stir in the **Flavorings** (except fresh ones) and cook to blend the flavors, about 1 minute longer. Remove the vegetables from the heat and set aside, uncovered, until the pasta is done.

3. Reserving 1 cup of the cooking liquid, drain the pasta and return to the pot. Add the contents of the skillet, some of the reserved cooking liquid, any fresh **Flavorings** and/ or **Enrichments,** and Parmesan cheese, tossing to coat. Taste, adjusting the seasonings, including pepper to taste. Serve, with additional cheese passed separately.

Note on Flavorings: This can be dried herbs, spices, or flavorings like nuts, capers, olives, or prosciutto, which cook with the vegetables. Fresh flavorings like herbs and zests are added at the end when tossing the Parmesan cheese with the pasta. See page 130 for ideas and general guidelines.

Note on pork rendering: If using pork rendering as the fat, first cook the bacon or sausage in a large skillet over medium-high heat until cooked. Remove the pork with a slotted spoon and set aside. Eyeballing the amount, drain the rendering or add more oil to equal 4 tablespoons. Using the same skillet, proceed with step 2.

Pasta with Mushrooms, Rosemary, and Garlic

Fresh rosemary is the exception to the fresh flavoring rule.

Vegetables: mushrooms
Fat: olive oil
Aromatic: garlic
Flavorings: 1½ tablespoons minced fresh rosemary, 2 tablespoons minced fresh parsley leaves
Enrichment: 1 cup ricotta cheese or 4 beaten eggs

Follow the Pasta with Tender Vegetables technique, adding the rosemary in step 2 when instructed to add Flavorings and the parsley when instructed to add fresh Flavorings.

Pasta with Bell Peppers, Capers, and Basil

Vegetables: multicolored bell peppers
Fat: olive oil
Aromatic: onion
Flavorings: 2 tablespoons drained capers
Enrichment: ¼ cup pesto

Pasta with Sausage, Eggplant, Tomato, and Italian Seasoning

To make this dish vegetarian, substitute a can of drained white beans for the sausage and use olive oil to sauté the garlic.

Vegetables: eggplant
Fat: ¼ cup rendered sausage fat from ½ pound bulk Italian sausage
Aromatic: garlic
Flavorings: 1 teaspoon Italian seasoning, ¼ cup minced fresh parsley leaves
Enrichment: 1 cup Simple Tomato Sauce (page 117) or good-quality jarred marinara

Pasta with Zucchini, Tomato, and Oregano

Vegetables: zucchini
Fat: olive oil
Aromatic: onion
Flavorings: ½ teaspoon dried oregano
Enrichment: 1 cup Simple Tomato Sauce (page 117) or good-quality jarred marinara

Pasta with Fennel, Red Onion, Walnuts, and Parsley

Vegetables: fennel
Fat: olive oil
Aromatic: red onion
Flavorings: ¼ cup toasted chopped walnuts, ¼ cup minced fresh parsley leaves
Enrichment: 1 cup ricotta cheese

At a Glance

PASTA WITH TENDER VEGETABLES

1. Internalize the formula: 12 ounces pasta, a generous 1 pound vegetables, 4 tablespoons fat, aromatic (garlic or onion), flavorings, and optional enrichments—and don't forget the Parmesan cheese!

2. Know the technique: Cook the pasta. Reserving 1 cup of the cooking water, drain the pasta and return it to the pot.

3. Cook the garlic in the fat until it starts to sizzle or sauté the onion until it starts to soften.

4. Add the tender vegetables and sauté until just softened. Stir in the flavorings (except fresh ones).

5. Toss the drained pasta with the contents of the skillet, fresh flavorings and/or enrichments (if using), Parmesan cheese, and cooking liquid as needed. Adjust the seasonings.

Make It
Pizza Night

There was a time when I'd buy store-bought crust to
make pizza, but since pizza has become our family's
signature dish—the meal family members
request for birthday dinners and celebrations—I can't
bring myself to buy crust anymore. As a result,
I've worked to streamline from-scratch pizza.

Pizza Formula

Short of owning a wood-fired pizza oven, *grilling* is the easiest and best way to make great pizza at home. My grill is located on a deck just a few steps away from my kitchen and hooked up to a gas line (as opposed to a small tank), so I grill pizza regularly year round, and since I do it often, grilling is as easy and familiar to me as turning on my oven. I know. I'm not the average cook.

But if you're able, grilling pizza is easier because once the grill preheats you've got a hot rack, a large surface, and a live fire ready to bake up to *four* large rectangles of dough at a time. And because the grill opens up (not out like an oven) it's less awkward. With a little practice, it's possible to lay up to four stretched rectangles of dough on the hot rack at the same time rather than sliding them on, one at a time, with a pizza peel.

It's possible to make great pizza in your oven, too. Rather than buy a pizza stone, most of which are large enough to bake only one pizza at a time, line your entire oven rack with either unglazed quarry tiles or unglazed stone tiles, either of which are inexpensive and available at tile shops or big-box home improvement stores.

Of course, there are those nights when you don't have time to do anything except top a store-bought crust, and that's okay. Whatever you make at home will always be better for you than take-out or anything from the frozen food case.

4 HOMEMADE PIZZA CRUSTS (OR 2 LARGE STORE-BOUGHT PIZZA ROUNDS)

Rethinking how to shape the dough and when to top the pizza are the first two steps in simplifying from-scratch pizza. It's much easier to stretch dough into a rough rectangle than a round. Plus, this shape bakes up crisper—no more limp pizza triangle tips.

To stretch dough, gently turn the risen dough from the bowl onto a floured surface. Avoid your instinct to punch it down, which causes the gluten to seize up, making it difficult to stretch until it relaxes again, another 15 to 20 minutes later. To form a rectangle, quarter the dough and then pick up a portion with both hands and pull it like you're stretching a piece of gum. The long, thin shape makes it possible to fit up to four pizzas at a time on a large grill or two pizzas in the oven—twice what you'd be able to fit with the round shapes.

Most pizza recipes instruct to top raw pizza dough, but it's easier to transfer *un-topped* stretched dough onto a hot grill or into a tile- or stone-lined oven. And naked stretched dough bakes or grills up brown on the bottom and blond on the top in just minutes. Parbaked or par-grilled pizzas are easier to top and transfer, and they cook up—crisped bottom and cheese-melted top—in just another few minutes. Grilling or baking untopped dough means you can make the crusts ahead and top them at your leisure.

GRILLED PIZZA CRUSTS

Makes 4 pizzas (serves up to 8)

This pizza dough formula is similar to Daily Bread (page 71). The only difference is a couple of tablespoons of olive oil and a couple of teaspoons of sugar added to the pizza dough to help it crisp up and brown better. If you memorize the bread formula, and then remember to add 2 tablespoons olive oil and 2 teaspoons sugar, you've got your pizza dough down, too.

⅓ cup warm water and 1⅓ cups room temperature water

2 teaspoons (or 1 envelope) active dry yeast

2 tablespoons extra-virgin olive oil

4 cups bread or unbleached all-purpose flour

2 teaspoons table salt

2 teaspoons sugar

Cornmeal, for the baking sheets

---

1. Measure the ⅓ cup warm water in a 2-cup measuring cup. Whisk the yeast into the water and let stand until foamy, just a few minutes. Add the remaining 1⅓ cups water and the oil to the yeast mixture.

2. Meanwhile, pulse the flour, salt, and sugar in a large food processor fitted with a steel blade.

3. Pour the liquid ingredients over the flour and process to form a rough soft ball. If the dough does not come together, add additional water, a couple of teaspoons at a time. Continue to machine-knead the dough until smooth, about 30 seconds longer. Turn the dough onto a floured surface and knead a few seconds to form a smooth ball. Coat a large bowl with vegetable cooking spray, add the dough, and cover with a damp kitchen towel. Let rise in a warm spot until doubled in size, about 2 hours.

4. When ready to make the pizzas, turn all burners of a gas grill on high until very hot, about 10 minutes. Without punching the dough down, dump it onto a lightly floured surface. Using a chef's knife or a metal dough scraper, quarter the dough. Working one at a time, stretch each portion into a rustic 12 × 3½- to 4-inch rectangle; transfer to 1 of 2 large cornmeal-coated baking sheets. Repeat with the remaining portions of dough. (The dough can also be punched down and refrigerated for up to 3 days, and is immediately ready to stretch.)

5. Carefully lift the stretched pieces of dough and lay them on the hot grill grate. Cover and grill until the bottoms are spotty brown, moving them around to ensure even cooking, and piercing the puffing dough as necessary, 2 to 3 minutes, depending on heat intensity. Turn the pizzas over and continue to grill, covered, until spotty brown on the second side, a couple of minutes longer. Remove the pizza crusts from the grill. (Crusts can be wrapped tightly and frozen for several months.)

OVEN-BAKED PIZZA CRUSTS

Makes 4 large pizzas (serves up to 8)

Dough from Grilled Pizza Crusts (page 151)

1. Make the dough and let rise as directed in steps 1, 2, and 3.

2. When ready to make pizzas, remove all but 1 oven rack and adjust it to the lowest position. Line the rack with quarry- or stone-tiles. Heat the oven to 550°F, letting the tiles continue to heat 15 minutes after the oven has reached temperature.

3. Shape the pizzas as directed in step 4. Working with 2 at a time, place each portion of stretched dough on a large *unrimmed* baking sheet generously sprinkled with cornmeal and slide them onto the heated tiles. (You should be able to bake 2 crusts at a time.) Bake until the crust bottoms are browned, 3 to 4 minutes. Remove from the oven and repeat with the remaining 2 portions of dough.

TIPS AND TRICKS

- If you make a lot of pizza and bread, buy yeast in bulk and store it in the freezer, where it lasts much longer than the suggested expiration date.

- If serving fewer than 4 people, bake all 4 crusts and wrap and freeze the remaining crusts for a quick dinner down the road.

- It's okay to buy pizza dough. To make 4 pizzas, purchase 2 pounds of dough and follow the shaping instructions in step 4 of Grilled Pizza Crusts (page 151). Then either grill or oven bake the stretched dough.

ITALIAN-INSPIRED PIZZA SAUCES

I rarely sauce or top all 4 pizzas the same way, but the sauce quantities listed below are enough for all 4.

TRADITIONAL (2 cups, enough for 4 pizzas)

- **Simple Tomato Sauce (page 117)**
- **No-Cook Red Sauce:** Mix 2 cups canned crushed tomatoes, 2 large garlic cloves, minced, and 1 tablespoon extra-virgin olive oil.
- **No-Cook White Sauce:** Mix 2 cups part-skim ricotta, ¼ cup milk, 2 large garlic cloves, minced, and a generous sprinkling of salt and pepper.

OTHER "SAUCING" OPTIONS

- **Fresh Red "Sauce":** Thinly slice 12 Campari tomatoes, lightly drizzle with extra-virgin olive oil, and season with salt and pepper.
- **Prepared Pesto:** Use 1⅓ cups.
- **Mozzarella:** Thinly slice 12 ounces regular or smoked mozzarella. (If you choose mozzarella as your base, you'll need an additional grated cheese for topping; (see "Melting Cheeses," page 158).

For saucing just one pizza, you'll need:

- ½ cup Simple Tomato Sauce, No-Cook Red Sauce, or No-Cook White Sauce
- 3 thinly sliced Campari tomatoes sprinkled with salt and lightly drizzled with olive oil
- ⅓ cup pesto
- 3 ounces regular or smoked mozzarella, thinly sliced

Butternut Squash–Red
Onion Pizza

Wild Mushroom Pizza

White Bean–Broccoli Rabe Pizza

Toppings: 1 Cup— More or Less—Per Pizza

Sometimes it's worth buying specific pizza toppings. More often, though, you can just open the fridge and see what's there. If you've got cooked vegetables, use them. If not, thinly slice or finely dice fresh ones, tossing them with a little olive oil, salt, and pepper. Of course, you can make a single-topping pizza—mushroom or pepperoni, for example—but I tend to go for two. There are a few exceptions (see below), but just remember you need about 1 cup toppings per pizza (4 cups total).

PROTEIN

If you're making a two-topping pizza and one of those toppings is protein, figure ½ cup per pizza of one of the following. Two exceptions to the rule: ⅓ cup bacon per pizza is probably enough, and since there's only ⅓ cup clams in a 6.5-ounce can, there's no point opening a second one to make the ½ cup.

- Shredded cooked chicken tossed with BBQ sauce
- Medium peeled raw shrimp, diced and tossed with a light olive oil drizzle
- Cooked bulk Italian Sausage Crumbles (page 64) or cooked links, thinly sliced
- Cooked ground meat (lamb, beef, or turkey) seasoned with salt and pepper
- Thin-sliced pepperoni
- Ham, cut into small dice
- Fried bacon bits (since it cooks again, I tend not to fry it up too crisp). Use only ⅓ cup.
- White beans, drained and tossed with a light olive oil drizzle (and no one would complain if you added a little minced garlic)
- 1 can (6.5 ounces) clams, drained, tossed with a light olive oil drizzle

VEGETABLES

If topping pizza with just vegetables, figure about 1 cup total of any bite-size vegetables— cooked or raw—for each pizza. Or if also topping with protein, reduce vegetables to ½ cup. If you've already got grilled, roasted, steam-sautéed or sautéed vegetables on hand (see "A Little Mise," page 34), use those.

TENDER VEGETABLES

Most vegetables are fine either raw or cooked, with the exception of mushrooms (see below). Cooked vegetables can go on as is. Toss prepared raw vegetables with a light olive oil drizzle and a sprinkling of salt and pepper and scatter over the sauced pizza crust.

- **Bell pepper** (**any color**): Thinly slice into short strips.
- **Red onion:** Peel, quarter, and thinly slice.
- **Mushrooms:** Thinly slice and cook. For 2 cups—enough for 2 pizzas—sauté 8 ounces mushrooms in 4 teaspoons hot oil in a large skillet until the moisture has evaporated and the mushrooms start to brown, about 5 minutes. Lightly season with salt and pepper.
- **Eggplant:** Cut into small dice.
- **Fennel:** Halve or quarter, core, and thinly slice.
- **Zucchini:** Halve or quarter lengthwise and thinly slice.

FIRM VEGETABLES

- **Asparagus:** Cut into 1-inch pieces; for medium to thick, thinly slice the pieces lengthwise.
- **Broccoli florets:** Cut into small florets.
- **Brussels sprouts:** Trim and thinly slice.
- **Winter squash, such as butternut:** Peel, seed, and thinly slice into bite-size pieces.
- **New potatoes** (**red or fingerling**) **or sweet potatoes:** Thinly slice (sweet potatoes may need to be halved or quartered, depending on size).

GREENS

Greens are different from other pizza toppings. They're very moist and would make a soggy single-topping pizza, so unless you precook them and squeeze out the excess moisture before topping the pizza, only use greens in combination with another topping or two. Also, because greens shrink a lot, figure 1 cup of raw greens per two-topping pizza.

- **Soft greens, such as arugula or baby kale or spinach:** Toss with a little olive oil, salt, and pepper and sprinkle over the pizzas as they emerge from the oven or grill.
- **Tender greens like beet greens, mature spinach, or Swiss chard:** Stem and wash, if necessary, tear into bite-size pieces, toss with a little olive oil, salt, and pepper and top pizzas *before* they go in the oven.
- **Sturdy greens, such as kale, turnips, collards, mustard, or broccoli rabe:** Stem and wash, if necessary, tear or chop into bite-size pieces, massage with a little olive oil, and then season with salt and pepper. Top pizzas *before* they go in the oven.

OTHER VEGETABLES

Thaw and toss with a couple of drops of olive oil.

- Frozen green peas

- Frozen corn

- Frozen or canned artichokes, cut into bite-size pieces

INTENSELY FLAVORED TOPPINGS: ¼ Cup—More or Less—Per Pizza

Because the following toppings are more intensely flavored, figure about ¼ cup rather than the usual ½ cup for a two-topping pizza.

- **Olives (especially Kalamata and oil-cured):** Pit and coarsely chop.

- **Caramelized Onions (page 51)**

- **Roasted peppers:** Thinly slice.

- **Prosciutto:** Two choices: Either top pizza with minced prosciutto *before* it goes in the oven, or lay thin slices of it over the pizza as it emerges from the oven.

- **Anchovies:** Mince or lay fillets on topped pizza.

MELTING CHEESES: A Generous ½ Cup Per Pizza

Cheese offers flavor, but it's also the culinary glue that holds the pizza together. Since crumbled cheeses like feta and goat offer great flavor but not a lot of melting power, consider mixing them with a mild melting cheese like mozzarella.

- Mozzarella, regular or smoked, thinly sliced or grated

- Provolone, grated and mixed with mozzarella

- Fontina, grated

- Asiago, grated

- Gruyère, grated and mixed with mozzarella

- Crumbled feta mixed with mozzarella

- Crumbled goat cheese mixed with mozzarella

- Crumbled blue cheese mixed with mozzarella

FINISHING HERBS AND SPICES

There's a restaurant near my house called Fat Cat's. Their pizzas are lean and simple, but what makes them special is the box of Penzey's spices they bring to the table along with the pizza. If you think sprinkling pizza with smoked paprika, cumin, or curry powder is weird, give it a try. Once you do, I'm betting you'll start setting out the spice box on pizza night, too. Here are some obvious—and not so obvious—choices.

- Red pepper flakes
- Aleppo pepper flakes
- Dried basil
- Dried oregano
- Smoked paprika
- Curry powder or garam masala
- Cumin
- Fennel pollen (or finely minced fennel seeds)
- Za'atar
- Sumac
- Soft fresh herbs: chopped basil, oregano, parsley, sage, mint, or snipped chives (or thinly sliced scallion greens)

CREATE-YOUR-OWN PIZZA

Makes 4 pizzas (serves up to 8 or 4 to 6 with leftovers)

This recipe assumes you are starting with precooked crusts—either homemade or store-bought.

---

4 Grilled or Oven-Baked Pizza Crusts (pages 151 and 152) or 2 large store-bought pizza crusts

2 cups **Pizza Sauce** (see page 153)

4 cups **Toppings** (see pages 156 to 158)

A generous 2 cups (8 to 10 ounces) **Melting Cheese** (see page 158)

Grated Parmesan cheese

Finishing Herbs/Spices (optional; see page 159)

---

1. If grilling the pizzas, turn the grill burners to low and heat to around 400°F. If oven-baking the pizzas, heat the oven to 425°F.

2. Top each pizza crust with a **Pizza Sauce,** scatter with 1 cup **Toppings** and ½ cup **Melting Cheese.**

3. For grilled: Lay the topped pizzas on the grill grates. Close the lid and grill until the pizzas are crisp-bottomed and the cheese has melted, about 5 minutes.

   For oven-baked: Place the pizza crusts on two large baking sheets and bake, rotating the pans and switching racks halfway through baking, about 10 minutes.

4. Transfer the pizzas to a cutting board and sprinkle with the Parmesan and **Finishing Herbs/ Spices** (if using), as each person desires. Cut and serve.

At a Glance

PIZZA

1. Make the dough or buy 2 pounds. Divide the dough and stretch each portion, then grill or bake. (Alternatively, start with store-bought crusts.)

2. Prepare the sauce, toppings, and cheese.

3. Assemble the pizzas, then grill or bake them.

4. Sprinkle with Parmesan and optional finishing herbs and spices.

Now that you've got the formula and the technique down, you probably don't need help putting together popular combos like sausage and pepper or mushroom and olive. The following are just a few interesting pizzas to get the creative juices flowing. If your fridge, freezer, and pantry are decently stocked, just open the doors and see what you've got.

Brussels Sprouts–Bacon Pizza

Diced ham is a fine stand-in if you don't have time to cook bacon.

Pizza Sauce: No-Cook White Sauce (page 153) or mozzarella cheese
Toppings: Brussels sprouts and bacon
Melting Cheese: Gruyère/mozzarella mix
Finishing Herbs/Spices: smoked paprika

Tomato, Corn, and Arugula Pizza

Pizza Sauce: Fresh Red "Sauce" (page 153)
Toppings: corn and arugula
Melting Cheese: mozzarella
Finishing Herbs/Spices: fresh or dried basil

Butternut Squash–Red Onion Pizza

Pizza Sauce: No-Cook White Sauce (page 153)
Toppings: butternut squash and red onion
Melting Cheese: provolone/mozzarella mix
Finishing Herbs/Spices: curry powder

Sausage-Fennel Pizza

Pizza Sauce: No-Cook White Sauce (page 153)
Toppings: Italian sausage and fennel
Cheese: mozzarella
Finishing Herbs/Spices: fennel pollen (or finely minced fennel seeds) and scallion greens

Spring Green Pizza

Pizza Sauce: No-Cook White Sauce (page 153)
Toppings: asparagus and peas
Cheese: Gruyère/mozzarella mix
Finishing Herbs/Spices: Sumac (optional) and scallion greens

Shrimp-Feta Pizza

Pizza Sauce: pesto
Toppings: shrimp and bell peppers
Cheese: mozzarella/feta mix
Finishing Herbs/Spices: dried oregano and/or za'atar

Confetti Pizza

Pizza Sauce: pesto
Toppings: multicolored peppers and red onion
Cheese: goat/Fontina mix
Finishing Herbs/Spices: za'atar or dried thyme

Wild Mushroom Pizza

Pizza Sauce: mozzarella
Toppings: sautéed mixed mushrooms
Cheese: Asiago
Finishing Herbs/Spices: dried thyme

White Bean–Broccoli Rabe Pizza

Pizza Sauce: No-Cook White Sauce, Simple Tomato Sauce, or No-Cook Red Sauce (pages 153, 117, and 153)
Toppings: ½ cup white beans and 1 cup massaged broccoli rabe
Cheese: provolone/mozzarella mix
Finishing Herbs/Spices: Aleppo pepper or red pepper flakes

Lamb-Feta Pizza

Pizza Sauce: Simple Tomato Sauce (page 117) or No-Cook Tomato Sauce (page 153)
Toppings: ground lamb or lamb sausage
Cheese: feta/mozzarella mix
Finishing Herbs/Spices: fresh mint and/or smoked paprika

Ham-Artichoke Pizza

Pizza Sauce: No-Cook White Sauce (page 153)
Toppings: ham and artichoke
Cheese: Gruyère
Finishing Herbs/Spices: chopped fresh parsley

Caramelized Onion–Olive Pizza

Pizza Sauce: Simple Tomato Sauce (page 117) or No-Cook Red Sauce (page 153)
Toppings: Caramelized Onions (page 51) and olives
Cheese: mozzarella
Finishing Herbs/Spices: dried thyme

GRILLED
PIZZA

Spring Green Pizza

Tomato, Corn, *and* **Arugula Pizza**

Sausage-Fennel Pizza

Weeknight Take-In

Stir-Fry,
Pad Thai, Lo Mein,
and Fried Rice

Dishing up sizzling vegetables and meat in a bright,
fresh sauce from a hot skillet beats poking at limp
vegetables in a gloppy sauce from a take-out box. So if
you can start to see Asian fast food as a formula
to internalize and a technique to master, you'll rarely
order take-out again.

Stir-Fry Formula

———

Long ingredients lists, lengthy preparation, and a foreign cooking process often make stir-fries seem impossible for weeknight cooking. For that very reason, I set out several years back to demystify stir-fry.

Working with that formula over the years, I've modified the recipe to make it even more supper-friendly, but the ingredient list is still virtually the same: 1 pound each protein and vegetables, 1 onion, 1 tablespoon each garlic and ginger, 1 recipe flavoring sauce, a little cornstarch diluted in water for thickener, and oil for stir-frying.

PROTEIN: 1 Pound

The following seafood, poultry, tofu, and cuts of meat require minimal preparation and cook quickly. Don't skip the marinating step—it makes a big difference in the balance of flavors. It doesn't need to marinate long—just make it the first thing you do in the process. Since domestic stoves just don't have the BTUs to sear large quantities at a time, you need to cook the meat in batches.

- **Peeled medium shrimp:** Pat dry.
- **"Dry" sea scallops (see page 190):** Pat dry and halve horizontally.
- **Boneless, skinless chicken breasts or thighs:** Cut into bite-size chunks or strips.
- **Pork tenderloin:** Thinly slice crosswise (if part of the tenderloin is very thick, halve it lengthwise before slicing).
- **Steak (sirloin, New York strip, rib eye, tenderloin):** Thinly slice across the grain and cut into bite-size pieces.
- **Flank or skirt steak:** Slice across the grain with the knife at a slight angle to the cutting board and cut into bite-size pieces.
- **Extra-firm tofu:** Pat dry. (If there's time, place on paper towels between 2 plates topped with a couple of cans.) Cut into bite-size chunks.
- **Tempeh:** Cut into bite-size pieces.

VEGETABLES: 1 Pound (Choose Two, ½ Pound Each)

For the same reason the protein must be cooked in batches, the vegetables must be added to the skillet incrementally. When choosing vegetables, pick one from the Firm Vegetables category and one from the Tender Vegetables category. This way you can lightly steam the firm vegetable before stir-frying, giving it a head start in the cooking process.

FIRM VEGETABLES (½ pound)

- **Asparagus:** Snap off ends and cut into 1-inch lengths. Halve thicker asparagus lengthwise.
- **Broccoli or cauliflower:** Trim and cut into bite-size florets (peel and slice broccoli stems).
- **Brussels sprouts:** Trim and halve lengthwise.
- **Carrots:** Peel and cut into bite-size slices. Halve thicker carrots lengthwise first.
- **Green beans:** Trim and cut into bite-size lengths. (Thin green beans or haricots verts are the best.)
- **Snow peas or sugar snap peas:** If not done already, remove strings.
- **Sweet potatoes:** Halve (or quarter if large) and cut into bite-size slices.
- **Winter squash, such as butternut:** Peel, seed, and cut into bite-size slices.

TENDER VEGETABLES (½ pound)

- **Bean sprouts:** Simply open the plastic bag and dump.
- **Bell peppers (yellow, red, and green):** Stem, seed, and slice into bite-size strips.
- **Cabbage:** Quarter, core, and shred thick.
- **Celery:** Cut into bite-size slices.
- **Corn, baby canned:** Drain and rinse (one 14-ounce can = 8 ounces, drained).
- **Eggplant:** Trim and cut into bite-size chunks.
- **Fennel:** Trim, halve, core, and shred thick.
- **Mushrooms, domestic white or baby bella:** Slice
- **Pineapple:** Peel, quarter, core, and cut into bite-size chunks. (This is not a vegetable, but it works like a tender vegetable.)
- **Water chestnuts, sliced canned:** Drain and rinse (one 8-ounce can = 5 ounces, drained).
- **Zucchini or yellow squash:** Trim and cut into bite-size slices. Halve or quarter large ones.

FLAVORING SAUCES: Choose 1

With the exception of the Basil (or Cilantro) Flavoring Sauce, which requires a fresh herb, **Flavoring Sauce** ingredients are simple pantry items. The sauces are mostly interchangeable and can be used with any of the stir-fry proteins and vegetables with the exception of Lemon-Coconut Flavoring Sauce, which is best paired with poultry, seafood, tofu, and tempeh.

With all of the **Flavoring Sauces,** just stir together. For a little extra kick, increase the pepper flakes from ¼ to ½ teaspoon.

General Tso's Flavoring Sauce

¼ cup dark soy sauce (or 2 tablespoons each molasses and soy sauce)

2 tablespoons rice vinegar

2 tablespoons sweet sherry

A generous ¼ teaspoon red pepper flakes

¼ cup water

Spicy Orange Flavoring Sauce

6 tablespoons orange juice concentrate

2 tablespoons dark soy sauce (or 1 tablespoon each soy sauce and molasses)

1 tablespoon toasted sesame oil

A generous ¼ teaspoon red pepper flakes

¼ cup water

Coconut Curry Flavoring Sauce

¾ cup coconut milk (light or regular)

2 tablespoons sweet sherry

2 tablespoons soy sauce

4 teaspoons light or dark brown sugar

2 teaspoons curry powder

Basil (or Cilantro) Flavoring Sauce

½ cup vegetable or chicken broth

¼ cup soy sauce

1 tablespoon rice vinegar

1 tablespoon sugar

⅓ cup chopped fresh basil or cilantro

Lemon-Coconut Flavoring Sauce

½ cup coconut milk (light or regular)

1 teaspoon finely grated lemon zest

3 tablespoons lemon juice

2 tablespoons soy sauce

2 tablespoons sweet sherry

4 teaspoons light or dark brown sugar

Sweet and Sour Flavoring Sauce

6 tablespoons pineapple juice

3 tablespoons soy sauce

3 tablespoons balsamic vinegar

1½ tablespoons light or dark brown sugar

A generous ¼ teaspoon red pepper flakes

Sichuan-Chili Flavoring Sauce

1 tablespoon soy sauce

1 tablespoon toasted sesame oil

1 tablespoon dark soy sauce

3 tablespoons sweet sherry

2 tablespoons chili garlic sauce or Sriracha sauce

½ teaspoon Sichuan peppercorns, crushed

¼ cup water

Stir-Fried Tofu *with* **Sugar Snap Peas** *and* **Baby Corn**

Stir-Fried Shrimp
with **Asparagus** *and*
Bean Sprouts

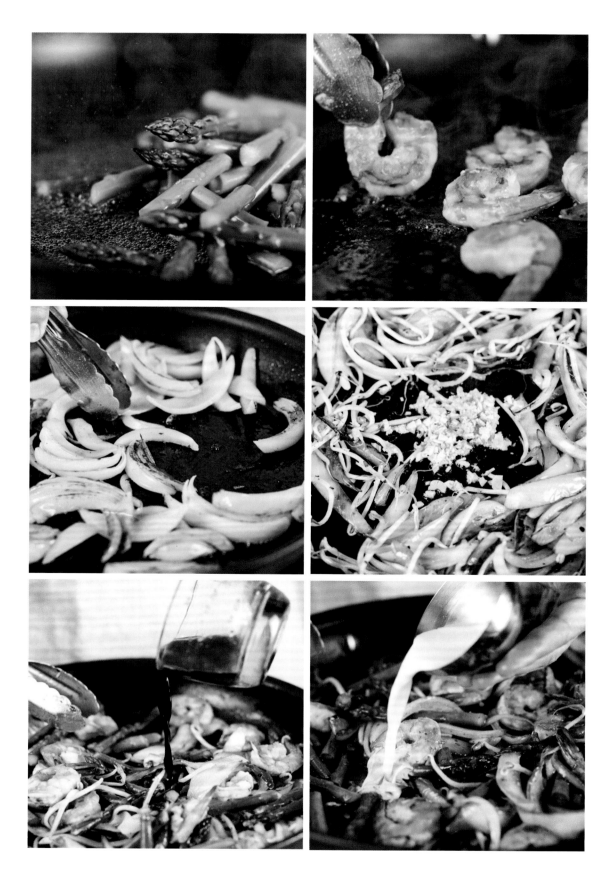

STIR-FRY

Serves 4

Once you've followed this technique a couple of times, you will internalize it. After that, you'll only need to refer to the **Flavoring Sauces.** Serve with Cooked White Rice or Cooked Brown Rice (page 61).

---

1 pound **Protein** (see page 165)

1 tablespoon soy sauce

1 tablespoon sweet sherry

½ pound **Firm Vegetables** (see page 166)

Salt

3 tablespoons peanut or vegetable oil

1 medium-large onion, peeled and halved from pole to pole, each half cut into 8 wedges

½ pound **Tender Vegetables** (see page 166)

1 tablespoon minced garlic (see Note)

1 tablespoons minced fresh ginger (see Note)

1 recipe **Flavoring Sauce** (see page 167)

2 teaspoons cornstarch mixed with 2 tablespoons water

Note: The quality of garlic and ginger paste in tubes in the produce department of many grocery stores is good and saves precious time.

---

1. Toss the **Protein** with the soy sauce and sherry in a medium bowl and set aside. Let the meat marinate while you prep all the vegetables and make the flavoring sauce.

2. When ready to cook, set a heavy-bottomed 12-inch skillet over low heat.

3. Place the **Firm Vegetables** in the skillet with a light sprinkling of salt and ¼ cup water. Cover the pan and increase the heat to high. When the water starts to steam, set the timer and cook until crisp-tender, 1 to 2 minutes: Figure 1 minute for delicate vegetables like asparagus and snow peas, 2 minutes for hardy vegetables like sweet potatoes and Brussels sprouts. Turn the vegetables into a large bowl.

4. Return the skillet to high heat and turn on the exhaust fan. Add 1 tablespoon oil and heat until wisps of smoke start to rise from the pan. Leaving any unabsorbed marinade in the bowl, and working in two batches, cook the **Protein,** turning once, until well browned and cooked through, 2 to 3 minutes per batch. Transfer the **Protein** to the bowl with **Firm Vegetables.**

5. Drizzle another 1 tablespoon oil into the hot skillet. Add the onion and stir-fry until spotty brown, 1 to 1½ minutes. Add the **Tender Vegetables** and stir-fry until crisp-tender, 1 to 1½ minutes longer. Make a well in the middle of the skillet and add the remaining 1 tablespoon oil, garlic, and ginger and cook until fragrant, a few seconds, then stir-fry into the vegetables. Return the steamed **Firm Vegetables** and the **Protein** to the skillet and stir-fry to heat through. Add the **Flavoring Sauce** and cook to coat all ingredients. Stir the cornstarch mixture and add it to the skillet. Cook until the juices become saucy and glossy. Serve immediately.

Stir-Fried Shrimp with Asparagus and Bean Sprouts

Protein: shrimp
Firm Vegetable: asparagus
Tender Vegetable: bean sprouts
Flavoring Sauce: Spicy Orange Flavoring Sauce (page 167)

Stir-Fried Scallops with Cauliflower and Celery (or Fennel)

Protein: scallops
Firm Vegetable: cauliflower
Tender Vegetable: celery
Flavoring Sauce: Lemon-Coconut Flavoring Sauce (page 167)

Stir-Fried Beef with Green Beans and Mushrooms

Protein: steak (your choice)
Firm Vegetable: green beans
Tender Vegetable: mushrooms
Flavoring Sauce: Sichuan-Chili Flavoring Sauce (page 167)

Stir-Fried Chicken with Winter Squash (or Carrots) and Cabbage

Protein: boneless, skinless chicken breasts or thighs
Firm Vegetable: winter squash or carrots
Tender Vegetable: cabbage
Flavoring Sauce: General Tso's Flavoring Sauce (page 167)

Stir-Fried Chicken with Broccoli and Peppers

Protein: boneless, skinless chicken breasts or thighs
Firm Vegetable: broccoli
Tender Vegetable: bell peppers
Flavoring Sauce: Basil Flavoring Sauce (page 167)

Stir-Fried Tofu with Sugar Snap Peas and Baby Corn

Protein: tofu
Firm Vegetable: snow peas
Tender Vegetable: baby corn
Flavoring Sauce: Coconut Curry Flavoring Sauce (page 167)

Stir-Fried Pork with Sweet Potatoes and Pineapple

Protein: pork tenderloin
Firm Vegetable: sweet potatoes
Tender "Vegetable": pineapple
Flavoring Sauce: Sweet and Sour Flavoring Sauce (page 167)

At a Glance

WEEKNIGHT STIR-FRY

1. Toss the protein with the soy sauce and sherry.

2. Prepare the onion and the firm and tender vegetables.

3. Prepare the garlic and ginger, mix the flavoring sauce, and dissolve the cornstarch.

4. Steam the firm vegetable and remove. Stir-fry the protein in two batches, followed by the onion, followed by the tender vegetable, then the garlic and ginger.

5. Return the cooked protein and the firm vegetable to the skillet.

6. Stir in the flavoring sauce and then the cornstarch mixture.

More Asian Fast Food:
Pad Thai, Lo Mein,
and Fried Rice

Although the flavorings and ingredients differ slightly, the methods for making lo mein and fried rice are almost identical. With cooked pasta or rice on hand, you can have lo mein or fried rice on the table in less than twenty minutes. As with stir-fry, the skillet must be searing hot, and the meat and vegetable additions are staggered so the ingredients stir-fry instead of stew.

Except for pineapple, which is good only in sweet-and-sour stir-fries, most of the suggested stir-fry meats or vegetables (see page 166) work equally well in lo mein or fried rice. Since the meat and vegetables are supporting rather than featured ingredients in these dishes, cut them slightly smaller than you would for stir-fry.

Although pad Thai doesn't quite offer the flexibility of ingredients that fried rice and lo mein do, the dish is definitely a close cousin. The technique is identical—keep the skillet hot, stagger the protein and vegetable additions, and add a cooked starch.

LO MEIN FLAVORING SAUCE

Enough to flavor one recipe lo mein

For a more kid-friendly dish, reduce the red pepper flakes to ½ or even ¼ teaspoon.

¼ cup chicken or vegetable broth

¼ cup soy sauce

2 teaspoons rice vinegar

2 teaspoons toasted sesame oil

1 teaspoon red pepper flakes

1 teaspoon sugar

Mix in a small bowl and set aside.

PAD THAI FLAVORING SAUCE

Enough to flavor 1 recipe Pad Thai

Thai or Vietnamese fish sauce, also known as nam pla or nuoc mam, is available at Asian specialty markets or in the Asian section of many grocery stores across the country.

---

6 tablespoons Thai or Vietnamese fish sauce

2 tablespoons sugar

1 teaspoon red pepper flakes

Mix all the ingredients, stirring until the sugar is dissolved.

PAD THAI

Serves 4

Pad Thai is made with rice noodles, which are cooked by simply pouring boiling water over them and letting them stand for a few minutes. The noodles can be drained and refrigerated in a zipper-lock bag for several days, making pad Thai especially easy to make. If you don't have or can't find rice noodles, you can use spaghetti or fettuccine in a pinch.

---

1 recipe **Pad Thai Flavoring Sauce** (page 173)

1 pound **Protein:** shrimp, chicken, or tofu, cut into bite-size pieces

3 tablespoons vegetable oil

1 medium onion, peeled and halved from pole to pole, each half cut in 6 to 8 wedges

1 bunch scallions, cut into 1-inch lengths, white and green parts reserved seperately

1 tablespoon minced garlic (or refrigerated paste)

4 cups cooked pad Thai noodles or spaghetti (8 ounces), patted dry

2 large eggs, lightly beaten

8 ounces (1 cup) bean sprouts, rinsed

1 lime, halved

¼ cup roasted peanuts, coarsely chopped

Chopped fresh cilantro leaves

---

1. Set a heavy-bottomed 12-inch nonstick or cast-iron skillet over low heat. Mix the **Pad Thai Flavoring Sauce.** Toss the **Protein** with 2 tablespoons of the flavoring sauce in a large bowl. Set aside while you prep the rest of the ingredients.

2. Three to 4 minutes before cooking, increase heat to high and turn on the exhaust fan. Add 1 tablespoon of the oil and heat until wisps of smoke start to rise from the pan. Working in two batches, stir-fry the **Protein,** turning once, until well browned and cooked through, 2 to 3 minutes per batch. Transfer the **Protein** to a clean bowl.

3. Add another 1 tablespoon of oil to the pan. Add the onion and stir-fry until spotty brown, 1 to 2 minutes. Stir in the scallion whites and garlic and cook until fragrant, a few seconds longer. Transfer the skillet contents to the bowl of protein.

4. Heat on high all but 1 teaspoon of the remaining oil to shimmering in the now-empty skillet. Add the noodles and stir-fry until heated through, about 2 minutes. Make a well in the center of the noodles and add the remaining oil and the eggs. Stir-fry the eggs until scrambled, about 1 minute. Return the **Protein** to the skillet. Add the remaining **Pad Thai Flavoring Sauce** and stir-fry until heated through.

5. Transfer the pad Thai to a large serving bowl. Add the bean sprouts and scallion greens, squeeze in half the lime, and toss to combine. Sprinkle with the peanuts and cilantro and serve immediately with the remaining half of the lime, cut into wedges.

At a Glance

PAD THAI

1. Have 4 cups of cooked pad Thai noodles on hand.

2. Heat a skillet over low heat while prepping, then increase to high 3 to 4 minutes before cooking.

3. Prepare the pad Thai flavoring sauce and marinate the protein in 2 tablespoons of it.

4. Cut the onion into wedges, mince the garlic, slice the scallions, beat the eggs, chop the peanuts, and slice the lime.

5. Stir-fry the protein in batches, followed by the onion, scallion whites, and garlic. Remove from the pan.

6. Stir-fry the noodles. Make a well and scramble in the eggs. Return the protein to the skillet and add the remaining pad Thai flavoring sauce.

7. Transfer to a serving bowl. Toss with the bean sprouts, scallion greens, and lime juice. Sprinkle with the peanuts and cilantro and serve with lime wedges.

LO MEIN

Chicken Lo Mein
with **Asparagus**
and **Water Chestnuts**

LO MEIN

Serves 4

If you're a cilantro fan and have the time, add a little chopped fresh to the finished dish.

½ pound **Protein** (see page 165)

1½ teaspoons soy sauce

1½ teaspoons sweet sherry

½ pound **Firm Vegetables,** cut into small bite-size pieces (see page 166)

Salt

2 tablespoons vegetable oil

½ pound **Tender Vegetables,** cut into small bite-size pieces (see page 166)

1 bunch scallions, sliced, white and greens parts reserved separately

1½ teaspoons minced garlic (or refrigerated paste)

1½ teaspoons minced fresh ginger (or refrigerated paste)

4 heaping cups cooked lo mein noodles or leftover spaghetti (about 8 ounces uncooked)

1 recipe **Lo Mein Flavoring Sauce** (page 173)

---

1. Toss the **Protein** with the soy sauce and sherry in a large bowl and set aside. Let the meat marinate while you prep all the vegetables and make the flavoring sauce.

2. When ready to cook, set a heavy-bottomed 12-inch nonstick or cast-iron skillet over low heat.

3. Place the **Firm Vegetables** in the skillet with a light sprinkling of salt and ¼ cup water. Cover the pan and increase the heat to high. When the water starts to steam, set the timer and cook until crisp-tender: Figure 1 minute for delicate vegetables like asparagus and snow peas, 2 minutes for hardy vegetables like sweet potatoes and Brussels sprouts. Turn the vegetables into a large bowl.

4. Return the skillet to high heat and turn on the exhaust fan. Add 1 tablespoon of the oil and heat until wisps of smoke start to rise from the pan. Leaving the unabsorbed marinade in the bowl, stir-fry the **Protein** until browned and cooked through, about 2 minutes. Add the **Tender Vegetables** along with the scallion whites and stir-fry until tender-crisp, 1 to 2 minutes. Stir in the garlic and ginger and cook until fragrant, a few seconds longer. Transfer the skillet contents to the bowl with the **Firm Vegetables.**

5. Add the remaining 1 tablespoon oil to the now-empty skillet and heat on high until shimmering. Add the noodles and stir-fry until heated through, about 2 minutes. Return the **Protein** and **Vegetables** to the skillet, along with the **Lo Mein Flavoring Sauce** and scallion greens. Stir-fry to combine and heat through. Serve immediately.

Shrimp Lo Mein with Snow Peas and Peppers

Protein: shrimp
Firm Vegetable: snow peas
Tender Vegetable: peppers

Lo Mein with Tofu, Broccoli, and Mushrooms

Protein: extra-firm tofu
Firm Vegetable: broccoli
Tender Vegetable: mushrooms

Chicken Lo Mein with Asparagus and Water Chestnuts

Protein: boneless, skinless chicken breasts or thighs
Firm Vegetable: asparagus
Tender Vegetable: celery stalks and water chestnuts

Pork Lo Mein with Butternut Squash and Cabbage

Protein: pork tenderloin
Firm Vegetable: butternut squash
Tender Vegetable: shredded cabbage

At a Glance
LO MEIN

1. Make sure to have 4 cups of lo mein noodles or cooked spaghetti.

2. Toss the protein with the soy sauce and sherry so it can marinate while you prep.

3. Prepare the scallions and the firm and tender vegetables.

4. Prepare the garlic and ginger and make the lo mein flavoring sauce.

5. Steam the firm vegetable and remove from the pan.

6. Stir-fry the protein, then the tender vegetable and scallion whites, then the garlic and ginger. Remove from pan and add to the firm vegetable.

7. Stir-fry the noodles. Return the protein and vegetables to the pan. Add the flavoring sauce and scallion greens and heat through.

FRIED RICE

Serves 4

The rice needs to stir-fry in a generous amount of oil. (It's fried rice, after all!) If you don't use enough, the dish starts to taste more like a rice casserole.

½ pound **Protein** (see page 165), cut into small bite-size pieces

1½ teaspoons plus 3 tablespoons soy sauce

1½ teaspoons sweet sherry

½ pound **Firm Vegetables** (see page 166)

Salt

4 tablespoons vegetable oil

½ pound **Tender Vegetables** (see page 166)

1 bunch scallions, sliced, white and greens parts reserved separately

1 large garlic clove, minced

4 cups cooked white or brown rice

2 large eggs, beaten

---

1. Toss the **Protein** with the 1½ teaspoons of the soy sauce and the sherry in a large bowl and set aside. Let it marinate while you prep all the rest of the ingredients.

2. When ready to cook, set a heavy-bottomed 12-inch nonstick or cast-iron skillet over low heat.

3. Place the **Firm Vegetables** in the skillet with a light sprinkling of salt and ¼ cup water; cover the pan and increase the heat to high. When the water starts to steam, set the timer and cook until crisp-tender, 1 to 2 minutes: Figure 1 minute for delicate vegetables like asparagus and snow peas, 2 minutes for hardy vegetables like sweet potatoes and Brussels sprouts. Turn the vegetables into a large bowl.

4. Return the skillet to high heat and turn on the exhaust fan. Add 1 tablespoon of the oil and heat until wisps of smoke start to rise from the pan. Leaving unabsorbed marinade in the bowl, stir-fry the **Protein** until browned and cooked through, about 2 minutes. Add the **Tender Vegetables** along with scallion whites and stir-fry until tender-crisp, 1 to 2 minutes. Stir in the garlic and cook until fragrant, a few seconds longer. Transfer the skillet contents to the bowl of **Firm Vegetables.**

5. Heat on high all but 1 teaspoon of the remaining oil to shimmering in the now-empty skillet. Add the rice and stir-fry until heated through, about 2 minutes. Make a well in the center of the rice and add the remaining 1 teaspoon oil and the eggs. Stir-fry until scrambled, about 1 minute. Return the **Protein** and the **Vegetables** to the skillet, along with the remaining 3 tablespoons soy sauce and the scallion greens. Stir-fry to combine and heat through. Serve immediately.

Fried Rice with Pork, Brussels Sprouts, and Mushrooms

Protein: pork tenderloin
Firm Vegetable: Brussels sprouts
Tender Vegetable: mushrooms

Fried Rice with Shrimp, Broccoli, and Water Chestnuts

Protein: shrimp
Firm Vegetable: broccoli
Tender Vegetable: 1 can
(8 ounces) sliced water chestnuts

Fried Rice with Tofu, Carrots, and Celery

Protein: extra-firm tofu
Firm Vegetable: carrots
Tender Vegetable: celery

Fried Rice with Chicken, Cauliflower, and Peppers

Protein: boneless, skinless chicken breast or thighs
Firm Vegetable: cauliflower
Tender Vegetable: bell pepper

TIPS AND TRICKS

- Cut protein and vegetables into small bite-size pieces for this dish.

- You can also use leftover meat, poultry, and shrimp: Figure 1½ to 2 cups.

- Toss in a handful of thawed frozen peas at the end, if you like.

- For a slightly different flavor, add 1½ tablespoons each soy sauce and fish sauce (as substitute for the 3 tablespoons soy sauce) at the end.

At a Glance
FRIED RICE

1. Make sure to have 4 cups of cooked rice on hand.

2. Toss the protein with soy sauce and sherry in a large bowl and let marinate while you prep.

3. Prepare the scallions, the firm and tender vegetables, and the garlic.

4. Steam the firm vegetable and remove it from the pan.

5. Stir-fry the protein, followed by the tender vegetable and scallion whites, followed by the garlic. Remove from the pan.

6. Stir-fry the rice. Make a well and scramble the eggs.

7. Return the protein and vegetables to the pan. Add the remaining soy sauce and scallion greens and heat through.

Fried Rice *with* Chicken, Cauliflower, *and* Peppers

If You've Made One Sear or Sauté, You've Made Them All

———

Given the choice between poached or seared scallops or poached or sautéed chicken breasts, I'll go for the dark crusty cuts every time. That rich brown surface not only looks great, but it's an indication of great flavor. Whip up a quick pan sauce and serve your cuts with a side of vegetables or on a salad, green beans, and/or grain, and you've got a restaurant-worthy meal any night of the week.

How to Sear

Whether you're searing a couple of chicken cutlets, a New York strip, a pan full of pork medallions, or a salmon fillet, the searing technique is the same: Get the skillet smoking hot (don't forget to turn on the exhaust fan!), lightly coat both sides of the cut(s) with oil, and season simply with salt and pepper.

CUTS FOR SEARING

You can sear just about any individual cut, from *thin* cuts you want fully cooked (chicken cutlets or pork medallions) to *thick* cuts you want medium-rare to medium (salmon fillets or beef steaks). Cooking times may vary a minute or two and pan size may change, but the technique is the same.

CHICKEN

2 large boneless, skinless chicken breasts
(10 to 12 ounces each), sliced horizontally into 2 cutlets each (for a total of 4)

Sautéing is the preferred method for chicken breasts, but if you halve them horizontally into two thin cutlets, you can crank up the heat and sear them in half the time and in half the fat. All you need is a sharp knife and a little confidence.

Following the Master Technique for Seared Cuts (page 195), cook the chicken cutlets for 5 minutes, turning them only once, after the first side has developed a rich brown crust, about 3 minutes.

1½ pounds boneless, skinless chicken thighs
(6 to 8 small/medium or 4 to 6 medium/large)

Compared with chicken breasts, chicken thighs are meatier and easier to cook. Whereas overcooked chicken breasts are tough and dry, it's nearly impossible to overcook a chicken thigh. Just like chicken breasts, chicken thighs vary in size. Figure 2 small/medium or 1 to 1½ medium/large chicken thighs per person.

Following the Master Technique for Seared Cuts (page 195), sear small/medium chicken thighs about 8 minutes, turning them only once, after the first side has developed a rich brown crust, about 4 minutes. Larger chicken thighs should be fully cooked in 10 minutes, so turn them after 5 minutes.

Seared Salmon *with*
Lemon-Caper Pan Sauce

Seared Scallops *with*
Orange-Balsamic Pan Sauce

FISH AND SHELLFISH

4 center-cut salmon fillets (about 6 ounces each)

Fillets near the tail are thin and easy to overcook, so unless you like well-done salmon, ask for thick center-cut fillets. Salmon fillets often come skinned, but if searing skin-on salmon, start it flesh side down. Otherwise, the skin pulls taut as it sears, causing the fillet to bow slightly and the flesh side to sear unevenly.

Following the Master Technique for Seared Cuts (page 195), sear salmon fillets for 7 minutes (for medium) to 8 minutes (for medium-well), turning them only once, after the first side has developed a rich brown crust, 3 to 3½ minutes. For thinner cuts, reduce cooking time on the flip side.

1½ pounds tuna, swordfish, shark, mahi-mahi, or other fish steaks, 1¼ to 1½ inches thick

Before buying seafood, check the Monterey Bay Aquarium Seafood Watch to see what's plentiful and what should be avoided. Like beef steaks, fish steaks should be thick enough so they don't overcook before both sides have seared. Better to buy odd-size thick fish steaks and divvy them up after cooking than four perfectly sized pieces that are too thin.

Following the Master Technique for Seared Cuts (page 195), sear fish steaks for 7 minutes (for medium) to 8 minutes (for medium-well), turning them only once, after the first side has developed a rich brown crust, 3½ to 4 minutes.

1½ pounds untreated or "dry" sea scallops

You can sear sea scallops in about 4 minutes, making them the ultimate, albeit expensive, fast food. Sea and bay scallops are often soaked in sodium tripolyphosphate, a preservative that not only masks the scallop's delicate, sweet flavor but results in a weight gain of up to 25 percent water weight, which starts to release as soon as they hit the skillet, causing them to steam rather than to sear. By law, treated scallops should be labeled as a "water-added scallop product," but if they aren't, ask.

Following the Master Technique for Seared Cuts (page 195), sear sea scallops for 4 minutes, turning them only once, after the first side has developed a rich brown crust, about 2 minutes.

PORK AND LAMB

1 to 2 pork tenderloins (1½ pounds total), cut into medallions

Unless you grill it, pork tenderloin is best cut into medallions and seared. Pat the tenderloin dry and cut crosswise into 1½-inch-thick medallions. Press each medallion with fingertips to ¾ to 1 inch thick.

Following the Master Technique for Seared Cuts (page 195), cook pork tenderloin medallions through in 7½ to 8 minutes, turning them only once, after the first side has developed a rich brown crust, 3½ to 4 minutes.

Loin lamb chops

Depending on appetites, figure 1 to 2 per person. If cooking 4 chops, use a 10-inch skillet. If cooking 8 chops, use a 12-inch skillet.

Following the Master Technique for Seared Cuts (page 195), cook lamb chops for medium-rare in 8 to 9 minutes, turning them only once, after the first side has developed a rich brown crust, about 4 minutes. (For medium, turn the heat to low and cook, turning once, for a couple of minutes longer.)

BONELESS BEEF STEAKS

When selecting a steak for searing, choose one of the following three boneless cuts. There are other great steaks to enjoy—skirt, flank, hanger—that have a long, thin shape that makes them better for grilling. Bone-in steaks are also better on the grill.

Strip steaks (aka New York strip, Kansas City steak, and strip loin or shell steak in Canada)

Figure two 12-ounce strip steaks 1 to 1¼ inches thick for 4 people.

Following the Master Technique for Seared Cuts (page 195), sear steaks for medium-rare to medium in 6 to 7 minutes, turning them only once, after the first side has developed a rich brown crust, about 3 minutes. (For a more well-done steak, turn the heat to medium-low and cook, turning once, a couple of minutes longer.)

Beef rib steaks (aka rib-eye steak or Delmonico)

Figure two 12-ounce rib steaks 1 to 1¼ inches thick for 4 people.

Following the Master Technique for Seared Cuts (page 195), cook steaks for medium-rare to medium in 6 to 7 minutes, turning them only once, after the first side has developed a rich brown crust, about 3 minutes. (For more well-done steaks, turn the heat to low and cook, turning once, a couple of minutes longer.)

Filet mignon

These steaks are cut from the long, tapered beef tenderloin and vary in size but are smaller and thicker than rib and loin steaks and will likely fit into a 10-inch skillet. Look for filets 1½ to 2 inches thick and in the 6-ounce range.

Following the Master Technique for Seared Cuts (page 195), cook filet mignons for medium-rare in 7 to 8 minutes, turning them only once, after the first side has developed a rich brown crust, 3½ to 4 minutes. (For medium filets, turn the heat to low and cook, turning once, for a couple of minutes longer.)

GROUND MEAT

1¼ to 1½ pounds ground beef (chuck if you can find it) or ground lamb

Burgers are searing candidates, too. When prepared with the right grind of meat, formed with a light hand, and seared properly, a well-made burger rivals a great steak. Forget the buns and ketchup. All this burger needs is a pan sauce and a glass of red wine.

The only difference between burgers and other cuts of meat is how you season them. Rather than oiling and seasoning the meat's surface with salt and pepper, break up the ground meat in a bowl and season it with ¾ teaspoon salt and ¼ teaspoon ground black pepper—no oil necessary—tossing it lightly to distribute seasonings. Divide the meat into 4 equal portions, patting each lightly with fingertips to form patties 1 inch thick.

Following the Master Technique for Seared Cuts (page 195), cook burgers for medium-rare in 8 minutes and medium in 9 minutes, turning them only once, after the first side has developed a rich brown crust, 4 to 5 minutes. (For medium-well to well-done burgers, turn the heat to low and cook, turning once, a couple of minutes longer.)

Note: Where there's sizzle, there's splatter, and splatter screens notwithstanding, searing leaves a film. On sear nights, just squirt the stove with degreaser and wipe it clean. It's a small price to pay for wonderfully crusted meat, fish, and poultry.

MASTER TECHNIQUE FOR SEARED CUTS

Serves 4

If you need your pan hotter quicker, just preheat it on medium rather than low heat.

1½ pounds **Cuts for Searing** (see pages 187 to 193)

1½ tablespoons olive or vegetable oil

Salt and ground black pepper

Optional: All-Purpose Salsa (page 210), an uncooked relish (pages 210 to 211), or a pan sauce (pages 207 to 209)

Note: Thicker and smaller than the other cuts, filet mignons are the only cut that will fit in a 10-inch skillet.

---

1. Set a heavy-bottomed 12-inch skillet (see Note) over low heat for 5 to 10 minutes while preparing the meal and seasoning the **Cuts.** Three to 4 minutes before searing the **Cuts,** increase the heat to high and turn on the exhaust fan.

2. Set the **Cuts** on a plate, pat dry, and drizzle with oil, turning to coat. Sprinkle both sides with salt and pepper.

3. A minute or so after the residual oils in the skillet send up wisps of smoke, put the **Cuts** in the pan. Cook until they develop an even, rich brown crust, 2 to 4 minutes (see specific cuts for details). Turn and continue to cook until the second side develops an even, rich brown crust and the cut is cooked to desired doneness, 2 to 4 minutes longer. Remove the **Cuts** to a plate and let rest a couple of minutes.

4. Serve with salsa or an uncooked relish, or make a pan sauce (see "Instant Gratification: Pan Sauces and Drizzles," pages 204 to 209).

At a Glance

HOW TO SEAR

1. Heat a heavy-bottomed skillet over low heat. Oil the cuts (not the pan!) and season both sides with salt and pepper.

2. Three to 4 minutes before searing, increase the heat to high and turn on the exhaust fan.

3. Cook the cuts, without turning, until a rich brown crust forms, 2 to 4 minutes. Turn and repeat on remaining side, 2 to 4 minutes longer. (So you don't lose track of time, set a timer!)

4. Make a pan sauce or serve with salsa or an uncooked relish.

SEARED
CUTS

Seared Steak *with*
Pickled Pink Onions
(page 53)

Seared Pork Tenderloin Medallions *with* Balsamic Vinegar Pan Sauce

How to Sauté

I sear (and grill) a lot more than I sauté, but sautéing is still a useful technique and one every cook should master—especially for delicate cuts like fish fillets and thicker cuts that need to cook through, such as boneless, skinless chicken breasts and pork chops. The cooking times vary slightly, but regardless of the cut, the technique is the same.

Searing and sautéing are similar techniques, but there are three key differences: 1. Heat level. 2. How the cut is prepared. 3. Where you put the fat. Searing uses high heat and sautéing uses medium-high heat. Seared cuts are not dredged in flour or cornmeal, while sautéed cuts generally are. With searing, you rub the cut with oil and cook it in a dry, hot skillet, and with sautéing, you heat the fat in the skillet.

CUTS FOR SAUTÉING

4 small skinless, boneless chicken breasts (6 to 8 ounces each)

These days it's rare that chicken breasts come with that little strip of meat called the tenderloin still attached. If so, this delicious little nugget prevents the breast from cooking evenly, so pull it from each breast half, remove the tendon and sauté them separately. If the tenderloins have already been removed, boneless skinless breast halves require no preparation except a light pounding (your fist works well!), until they are more or less an even thickness.

Following the Master Technique for Sautéed Cuts (page 201), cook chicken breasts 6 to 7 minutes, turning them only once, after the first side is an impressive golden brown, 3½ to 4 minutes.

4 boneless pork loin chops, 1 to 1¼ inches each (about 6 ounces each)

Most cooks end up overcooking bone-in pork chops to get the meat nearest the bone done. For this reason, stick with boneless pork chops, preferably 1 to 1¼ inches thick. If the chops in the meat case are thin, buy a small boneless loin roast from the more flavorful, rosier-fleshed rib end and cut it into 1-inch-thick boneless chops. Better to split one thick chop between two people than to overcook two thin ones.

Following the Master Technique for Sautéed Cuts (page 201), cook 1-inch-thick boneless loin chops for 6 to 7 minutes, turning them only once, after the first side is impressively golden brown, 3½ to 4 minutes.

2 to 4 white-fleshed fish fillets, such as flounder, catfish, snapper, tilapia, grouper, or cod (1½ pounds total)

Fish fillets come in all sizes. Just know that you're looking for about 1½ pounds total. Cut larger fillets into individual portions before cooking, which will make them easier to turn in the pan. If the fish has skin, score it to keep the fillet from curling during cooking.

For sautéing, look for fish fillets ½ inch to 1¼ inches thick. Avoid fillets less than ½ inch thick, which overcook before they start to brown and also easily fall apart. You can buy fish fillets over 1¼ inches thick, but simply cut them crosswise into 1-inch-thick medallions.

Since most fish fillets are wider and thinner than the average chicken breast or pork chop, they take up more space in the skillet. You may need to cook them in two batches, meaning less fat and less mess.

Following the Master Technique for Sautéed Cuts (page 201), arrange 2 fish fillets in the skillet. Cook until a light golden brown crust forms, 2 to 3 minutes. Turn with a thin metal spatula and continue to cook until light golden brown on the other side, 1 to 3 minutes longer, depending on the thickness. Transfer the fish to a plate and set in a warm oven. Add the remaining fish, adding a little more oil to the skillet, if necessary, and repeat the sautéing process.

MASTER TECHNIQUE FOR SAUTÉED CUTS

Serves 4

Butter helps the cuts brown better, but if you like, you can just use 3 tablespoons olive oil.

¼ cup flour or fine cornmeal measured into a shallow pan

2 tablespoons butter

1 tablespoon olive oil

1½ pounds **Cuts for Sautéing** (see pages 198 to 199)

Salt and ground black pepper

Optional: All-Purpose Salsa (page 210), an uncooked relish (pages 210 to 211), or a pan sauce (pages 207 to 209)

Lemon wedges

---

1. Spread the flour or cornmeal in a shallow pan.

2. Heat the butter and oil in a large skillet over medium-low heat. While the pan is heating, sprinkle **Cuts** on both sides with salt and pepper and then dredge in the flour or cornmeal.

3. A couple of minutes before sautéing, increase the heat to medium-high. When the butter stops foaming and starts to smell nutty, arrange the **Cuts**, presentation side (if there is one) down. Cook, turning only once, until rich golden brown, 2 to 3 minutes per side (see specific cuts for details). Remove from the skillet and serve with lemon wedges. Alternatively, serve with salsa or relish, or make a pan sauce. (See "Instant Gratification: Pan Sauces and Drizzles," pages 204 to 209).

At a Glance
HOW TO SAUTÉ

1. Heat butter and oil in a large skillet over medium-low heat.

2. Season both sides of the cuts with salt and pepper, then dredge in flour or cornmeal.

3. A few minutes before sautéing, increase the heat to medium-high.

   When the butter turns golden brown and smells nutty, add the cuts.

4. Cook the cuts, turning only once, until golden brown on each side.

5. Make a pan sauce or serve with salsa or an uncooked relish.

**Sautéed Chicken Breast
over Lemony Lima Bean
and Rice Salad
with Cilantro-Lime Dressing**

Instant Gratification:
Pan Sauces and Drizzles

The simplest way to flavor your cut and simultaneously clean your skillet is to make a quick pan sauce. Whether searing or sautéing, the method is the same: Remove the sautéed or seared cuts from the pan, pour in ¾ cup liquid, which gets reduced by half within a couple of minutes, then stir in an enrichment—butter, olive oil, or heavy cream—and serve. That's all it takes to take dinner from ordinary to memorable.

Pan Sauce Formula

LIQUIDS

- **Juices and sweet fortified wines:** Marsala, Madeira, vermouth, and port all make fine sauces on their own. Reduce a straight ¾ cup of any of these liquids in a pan of drippings, and you'll get a decent sauce.

- **Wine:** Though not harsh, pan sauces made with straight red or white wine taste weak, sour, and off kilter. Cutting the wine with an equal amount of low-sodium chicken broth and whisking in a smidgen of Dijon mustard balances the sauce. For wine sauces, use equal parts (6 tablespoons each) chicken broth and wine.

- **Acidic liquids:** Sharp liquids like lemon juice or vinegar need taming; a sauce made with them would be too harsh. For these sauces, use a ratio of 1:3 lemon juice or vinegar to chicken broth, fortified wine, or juice. For example, for the ¾ cup (12 tablespoons) called for, use 3 tablespoons lemon juice or vinegar and 9 tablespoons broth/wine/juice. There are, of course, exceptions to the rule. Because balsamic vinegar is sweeter than other vinegars, figure equal parts chicken broth and balsamic. Asian-Style Sweet and Sour Pan Sauce (page 209) calls for 6 tablespoons chicken broth, 3 tablespoons soy sauce, and 3 tablespoons rice vinegar, rather than 9 tablespoons chicken broth and 3 tablespoons vinegar (but still a total of ¾ cup liquid).

FLAVORINGS

Pan sauce flavorings are optional, but if you have time, toss in one or more of the following. It adds textural and flavor interest to an already delightful little sauce (see suggestions on pages 208 to 209 for more inspiration).

- A handful of chopped nuts
- A handful of dried fruit
- A scattering of olives, capers, or sun-dried tomatoes
- A sprinkling of fresh herbs, dried herbs, or citrus zests

ENRICHMENTS

Once the sauce reduces by half—just eyeball it—it's time to enrich it. While the pan sauce should be light, one without a little fat is brash and intense. Not only does the fat enrich and soften the flavors, but it also thickens the sauce, giving it much-needed body. A small amount of sauce requires only a very small amount of fat, but that small addition can take a sauce from puckery to pleasant.

- 1 tablespoon butter
- 1 tablespoon olive oil
- 2 tablespoons heavy cream

PAN SAUCE

Makes enough for 4 seared or sautéed cuts

¾ cup **Liquids** (page 204)
Flavorings (optional; page 205)
Enrichments (page 205)

Mix the **Liquids** and **Flavorings** (if using) in a measuring cup. Once the seared or sautéed cut has been removed from the skillet, add the liquid to the empty skillet. Boil until reduced by half. Tilt the skillet so that the reduced liquid is at one side of the pan and whisk in the **Enrichment** until the sauce is smooth and glossy. Spoon a portion of sauce over each seared or sautéed cut and serve immediately.

TIPS AND TRICKS

- Be careful when adding the pan sauce liquid to the hot skillet. Pour the liquid into the pan from the side. If the pan is smoky hot, first remove it from the heat, then add the liquid.

- You can make the pan sauce ahead and let it sit while serving a salad or first course. When ready to serve, just heat it back up, adding a little water, if necessary, to bring it back to sauce-like consistency.

Red Wine Pan Sauce

For chicken and turkey cutlets, boneless pork chops and tenderloin, steaks and burgers.

Liquid: 6 tablespoons each chicken broth and full-bodied red wine
Flavorings: A generous teaspoon Dijon mustard
Enrichment: 1 tablespoon butter

Marsala Wine Pan Sauce with Figs and Pistachios

For poultry and pork.

Liquid: ¾ cup Marsala wine
Flavorings: ¼ cup coarsely chopped dried figs and 2 tablespoons coarsely chopped pistachios
Enrichment: 1 tablespoon butter

Sweet and Sour Vermouth Pan Sauce with Walnuts and Prunes

For poultry and pork.

Liquid: 9 tablespoons sweet vermouth or cream sherry and 3 tablespoons cider vinegar
Flavorings: ¼ cup chopped prunes and 2 tablespoons chopped walnuts
Enrichment: 1 tablespoon butter

Port Wine Pan Sauce with Dried Cherries (or Cranberries)

For poultry and pork.

Liquid: ¾ cup port wine
Flavorings: ¼ cup dried cherries or cranberries and 2 teaspoons cherry jam
Enrichment: 1 tablespoon butter

Tomato-Tarragon (or Rosemary) Pan Sauce

For fish, shellfish, poultry, pork, steaks, or burgers.

Liquid: 6 tablespoons each low-sodium chicken broth and dry vermouth or white wine
Flavorings: ¾ cup drained canned diced tomatoes (or equal amount diced Italian plum tomatoes) and ½ teaspoon dried tarragon or minced fresh rosemary
Enrichment: extra-virgin olive oil or butter

Provençal Tomato Pan Sauce with Black Olives and Provençal Herbs

For chicken and turkey cutlets, steaks, burgers, boneless pork chops and tenderloin, and fish steaks. Use dried thyme in a pinch.

Liquid: 6 tablespoons each low-sodium chicken broth and dry white wine
Flavorings: ¾ cup drained canned diced tomatoes (or equal amount diced Italian plum tomatoes), 2 minced garlic cloves, ½ teaspoon herbes de Provence, and 2 tablespoons coarsely chopped Kalamata olives
Enrichment: 1 tablespoon extra-virgin olive oil

White Wine Vinegar Pan Sauce

For chicken and turkey cutlets, fish fillets and steaks, and scallops.

Liquid: 9 tablespoons low-sodium chicken broth and 3 tablespoons white wine vinegar
Flavorings: 2 tablespoons Dijon mustard
Enrichment: 1 tablespoon butter

Balsamic Vinegar Pan Sauce

This pan sauce works for any cut.

Liquid: 6 tablespoons each balsamic vinegar and low-sodium chicken broth
Flavorings: None necessary, but dried fruit, nuts, and capers are nice
Enrichment: 1 tablespoon butter or extra-virgin olive oil

Balsamic Pan Sauce with Pine Nuts and Raisins

For poultry and pork.

Liquid: 6 tablespoons each balsamic vinegar and low-sodium chicken broth
Flavorings: ¼ cup raisins and 2 tablespoons toasted pine nuts
Enrichment: 1 tablespoon butter or extra-virgin olive oil

Apple Cider Pan Sauce

For chicken and turkey cutlets, boneless pork chops and tenderloin, and duck breasts.

Liquid: 9 tablespoons apple cider or juice and 3 tablespoons balsamic or cider vinegar
Flavorings: none necessary
Enrichment: 1 tablespoon butter

Orange-Dijon Pan Sauce with Rosemary

For fish, seafood, poultry, and pork. When making this pan sauce for pork, you can add 1 tablespoon brown sugar if you like.

Liquid: ¾ cup orange juice
Flavorings: 1 teaspoon Dijon mustard and ½ teaspoon minced fresh rosemary
Enrichment: 1 tablespoon butter or extra-virgin olive oil

Orange Pan Sauce with Pernod

For poultry, pork, fish, and seafood.

Liquid: 6 tablespoons each low-sodium chicken broth and orange juice
Flavorings: 1 teaspoon finely grated orange zest and 1 tablespoon Pernod
Enrichment: 1 tablespoon butter

Orange-Balsamic Pan Sauce

For poultry, pork, fish, and shellfish.

Liquid: 9 tablespoons orange juice and 3 tablespoons balsamic vinegar
Flavorings: none necessary
Enrichment: 1 tablespoon butter or extra-virgin olive oil

Lemon-Caper Pan Sauce

For chicken, pork, fish, and shellfish.

Liquid: 9 tablespoons low-sodium chicken broth and 3 tablespoons lemon juice
Flavorings: 1 tablespoon drained capers
Enrichment: 1 tablespoon butter

Quick Velouté

For poultry, fish, and shellfish.

Liquid: 6 tablespoons each low-sodium chicken broth and dry vermouth
Flavorings: none necessary
Enrichment: 2 tablespoons heavy cream

Mustard Cream Pan Sauce

For all seared and sautéed cuts.

Liquid: ¾ cup low-sodium chicken broth
Flavorings: 2 tablespoons Dijon or coarse-grained mustard
Enrichment: 2 tablespoons heavy cream

Horseradish Pan Sauce

For fish, steaks, and burgers.

Liquid: 6 tablespoons each low-sodium chicken broth and dry vermouth or white wine
Flavorings: 2 tablespoons prepared horseradish
Enrichment: 1 tablespoon butter

Black Pepper Molasses Pan Sauce

For pork, steaks, and burgers. If you've got cooked bacon in your larder (see "A Little Mise," page 34), add a couple of tablespoons of minced bits for an extra-special sauce.

Liquid: 6 tablespoons each low-sodium chicken broth and full-bodied red wine
Flavorings: 2 tablespoons molasses and several grinds black pepper
Enrichment: 1 tablespoon butter

Curried Chutney Pan Sauce

For poultry and pork.

Liquid: 9 tablespoons low-sodium chicken broth and 3 tablespoons rice vinegar
Flavorings: 2 tablespoons prepared chutney and ¼ teaspoon curry powder
Enrichment: 1 tablespoon butter

Asian-Style Sweet and Sour Pan Sauce

For poultry, fish, and pork. Unlike the other sauces, this one does not have an enrichment. If you have scallions, sprinkle the sauced cuts with some.

Liquid: 6 tablespoons low-sodium chicken broth, 3 tablespoons distilled white rice vinegar, and 3 tablespoons soy sauce or Vietnamese fish sauce
Flavorings: 2 tablespoons brown sugar and 2 garlic cloves, minced
Enrichment: None

Relishes and Toppings

The relishes and toppings that follow work year round with almost any sautéed or seared meat, poultry, or seafood. The All-Purpose Salsa formula can be made with just about any fruit you have on hand. The other relishes are made mostly with pantry ingredients, so if you're well stocked, you should be able to make one of them without a trip to the store.

ALL-PURPOSE SALSA

Makes 2 cups

Depending on the ingredients, this salsa can be served with chicken breasts and thighs, pork tenderloin and chops, scallops, fish fillets and steaks, and steaks and burgers. This salsa works with any fruit, and the same formula also works when making a black bean and/or corn salsa (see Note).

1½ cups finely diced fruit (tomatoes, avocado, peaches, nectarines, grapes, oranges, grapefruits, apricots, plums, or pineapple)

¼ medium red onion, finely diced, or 2 large scallions, thinly sliced

¼ yellow or red bell pepper, finely diced

1 jalapeño pepper, seeded and minced

1 tablespoon chopped fresh cilantro or parsley leaves

2 tablespoons lime juice or rice vinegar

½ teaspoon cumin or chili powder (optional)

Salt and ground black pepper, to taste

Mix all the ingredients in a medium bowl. Let stand, if possible, for the juices to release and the flavors to blend, 5 to 10 minutes.

Note: For a black bean and corn salsa, use equal parts of corn and black beans for a total of 1½ cups.

PARSLEY RELISH WITH CAPERS AND CORNICHONS

Makes a generous ½ cup

For chicken breasts and thighs, pork tenderloin and chops, scallops, fish fillets and steaks, and steaks and burgers.

½ cup fresh parsley leaves, coarsely chopped

3 cornichons (see Note), thinly sliced, plus 1 teaspoon brine from the jar

2 tablespoons capers

½ medium shallot or 1 scallion, thinly sliced

¼ cup extra-virgin olive oil

Salt and ground black pepper to taste

Mix all the ingredients in a small bowl.

Note: 2 tablespoons finely diced baby dill pickle can be substituted for the cornichons

TOMATO RELISH WITH PINE NUTS, GREEN OLIVES, AND LEMON ZEST

Makes about 1 cup

For chicken breasts and thighs, pork tenderloin and chops, fish fillets and steaks, and steaks and burgers. When tomatoes are in season, substitute 4 Italian plum tomatoes for the canned ones.

---

4 canned tomatoes, coarsely chopped

2 garlic cloves, lightly smashed and thinly sliced

2 tablespoons extra-virgin olive oil

¼ cup loosely packed fresh parsley leaves

1 tablespoon toasted pine nuts

4 green olives, pitted and coarsely chopped

2 strips lemon zest (1 inch wide), very thinly slivered

Salt and ground black pepper, to taste

Mix all the ingredients in a medium bowl.

PICKLED PINK ONIONS

Makes 5 to 6 cups

See the recipe on page 53. This relish is great with fish fillets and steaks and beef steaks and burgers.

ROASTED PEPPER RELISH WITH OLIVES, CAPERS, AND ROSEMARY

Makes a scant 1 cup

For chicken breasts and thighs, pork tenderloin and chops, fish fillets and steaks, and steaks and burgers. This recipe can be easily doubled or even more, and it holds well in the refrigerator for at least a week.

---

4 medium garlic cloves, peeled

2 tablespoons extra-virgin olive oil

3 jarred roasted red peppers, cut into medium dice (½ cup total)

4 piquant black olives, such as Kalamata, pitted and quartered

1 teaspoon drained capers

2 teaspoons minced fresh rosemary leaves

Ground black pepper, to taste

---

1. Heat the garlic and olive oil in a small saucepan over low heat. When the garlic starts to sizzle and turn golden, remove from the heat. Remove the garlic from the oil, and when cool enough to handle, quarter each clove lengthwise.

2. Meanwhile, mix the remaining ingredients in a small bowl. Add the olive oil and garlic. Toss to coat and serve.

All-Purpose Salsa

Simple Sides

When I make seared or sautéed cuts at home—chicken cutlets, seared salmon, pork chops, steak—the plate just usually feels a little empty without a hearty side, and these potatoes and polenta are among my favorites. Crisp Potato Cake is the fastest, most delicious way I know to get a potato from the vegetable basket to the plate. The Very Simplest Mashed Potatoes is still one of my weeknight regulars. With no constant stirring required, Quick Polenta is way easier to cook up than traditional polenta, and even faster than boiling a box of pasta. All three of these are perfect accompaniments to any seared or sautéed cut.

CRISP POTATO CAKE

Serves 4

Use any size potatoes that you've got as long as they weigh about a pound. No need to peel the potatoes—just grate them, skin and all! You can hold the potato cake in the skillet over low heat until you are ready to serve it, just occasionally flip it from side to side. To make a potato cake for 2 people, halve the recipe and use a small (8-inch) skillet. To make a potato cake for 8 people, double the recipe and use a large (12-inch) skillet.

3 tablespoons butter and/or olive oil

1 pound (4 small) baking potatoes, scrubbed and grated on the large holes of a box grater

Salt and ground black pepper

1. Heat 2 tablespoons of the butter and/or oil over low heat in a medium (10-inch) skillet. While the fat heats, grate the potatoes and, working with a small handful at a time, squeeze as much liquid from the potatoes as possible.

2. A minute or 2 before cooking, increase the heat to medium-high. Add the potatoes to the pan, pressing on them with a metal spatula to form a flat cake. Cook until the bottom of the cake is golden brown and crisp, about 4 minutes. Place a small plate over the pan and invert the cake onto the plate. Add the remaining 1 tablespoon of fat to the pan, and slide the cake back into the pan as soon as the fat heats. Continue to cook until golden brown on the remaining side, about 4 minutes longer. Reduce the heat to low and continue to cook until the cake bottom is crisp, about 2 minutes. Sprinkle with salt and pepper, cut into 4 wedges, and serve immediately.

THE VERY SIMPLEST MASHED POTATOES

Serves 4

1½ pounds potatoes (8 small red boiling potatoes or 12 little new potatoes)

4 tablespoons butter or extra-virgin olive oil

Salt and ground black pepper

Rough-chopped fresh parsley (optional)

1. Bring the potatoes and water to a boil in a large covered saucepan. Reduce the heat to medium-low and simmer until a paring knife inserted into the potatoes can be removed with no resistance, 25 to 30 minutes for medium potatoes or 15 to 20 minutes for new potatoes.

2. Drain potatoes, reserving ½ cup of the potato cooking liquid. Leave the cooked potatoes in the saucepan, slash them in half with a paring knife, and add the butter and ¼ cup of the reserved potato water along with a generous sprinkling of salt and pepper. Roughly crush potatoes with a fork, adding more water for desired consistency. Adjust seasonings, stirring in the parsley (if using). Serve immediately.

QUICK POLENTA

Serves 4

1 teaspoon salt

1 cup instant polenta

1 tablespoon butter

Ground black pepper

Bring 4 cups (1 quart) of water to a boil over medium-high heat in a large saucepan or small Dutch oven. Add the salt to the water and, while whisking constantly, add the polenta in a thin, steady stream. Continue to whisk until the polenta thickens to a soft but not soupy consistency, a couple of minutes. Remove the pan from the heat and stir in the butter and pepper to taste (and optional flavorings; see Note). Serve immediately.

Note: Stir any of the following flavorings into the cooked polenta:

¼ cup each of blue cheese and walnuts *or* 1 cup Fontina cheese and ¼ cup grated Parmesan *or* 1 cup fresh or frozen corn and ¼ cup grated Parmesan

Two Chickens, Three Dinners!

When I buy only one rotisserie chicken, it seems family
members compete for the two drumstick
and thigh portions, we squander the breast meat,
and I end up tossing the bones.

If I buy two rotisserie chickens, everyone gets a whole leg
for dinner the first night, leaving enough breast meat to
shred and flavor for another complete meal and the
bones and excess meat to make one or two pots of soup.
Three-plus meals is a way better deal!

Break 'Em Down

This is how two rotisserie chickens become multiple meals for the week:

- **The Legs:** While the rotisserie chickens are still warm, start by carving off the 4 drumsticks and thighs, leaving their skin intact. Chicken drumsticks and thighs taste best on the day they're roasted. For this reason, I try to serve them for dinner the same day. See Double-Roasted Chicken Legs (page 223), but if it's not possible to use the legs and thighs on the first day, it's OK, because the second roasting freshens them up nicely.

- **The Breasts:** Remove the skin from the breasts and toss it into a pot. Use a knife to remove the 4 breast halves from the bones and follow the shredding instructions under "The Chicken Breasts" on page 230.

- **The Bones:** Remove the excess meat from the chicken carcasses, add the remaining skin and bones to the pot, and follow the instructions in "The Broth" (page 225) to make a rich broth.

DIY Roast Chicken

Rather than buy two rotisserie chickens, you can roast your own two chickens, about 4 pounds each. Butterflying or splitting the birds down their backs and flattening them shaves nearly 30 minutes off the cooking process. Not only does butterflying save roasting time, but it also helps the chickens cook more evenly, ensuring the breast meat does not overcook and dry out.

If you're thinking ahead, it's nice to butterfly the chickens and salt them a day before roasting them, giving them time to absorb the salt so they taste seasoned throughout, not just on the surface.

If you want to roast them immediately, start by adjusting the oven rack to the upper-middle position and heating the oven to 450°F. After that, remove the giblet packets, rinse the chickens, and, working one at a time, split them down their backs with kitchen shears. Turn the chickens breast side up and use your palm or fist to flatten them. Pat the flattened chickens

dry. To ensure they brown well, place the butterflied chickens on a heavy-duty 18 × 12-inch rimmed baking sheet. Sprinkle both sides of the chickens all over with kosher salt (and pepper if you're roasting right away).

If roasting the chickens right away, rub them with a little olive oil and place them skin side up on the baking sheet. Roast until golden brown and the juices run clear, about 45 minutes. If you're waiting a day to roast them, set the pan in the refrigerator, uncovered. The next day, pepper and oil the chickens just before roasting.

One final benefit of butterflied chickens: They're easy to carve. The skin is all that's holding the legs to the breasts, so just give the legs a quick snip and serve the drumsticks/thighs for that night's dinner. When the chickens are cool enough to handle, remove and shred the breast meat, and place the remaining skin and bones in a large pot to make broth (see page 225).

Double-Roasted Chicken Legs
with **Hoisin Glaze**

The Legs

It's rare that I serve rotisserie chicken legs plain, especially when 5 minutes of effort and 12 minutes of additional roasting will make them taste so much more interesting. The second roasting actually refreshes the chicken legs, making them taste almost freshly roasted.

GLAZES

I've developed a few glazes to get you started (see page 224), but don't stop with these. If you've got peach preserves, apple butter, or cranberry sauce in the fridge, add a pinch of cloves and transform ho-hum rotisserie chicken legs into something special.

If you're wondering about the little cornstarch mixture, it helps the glaze cling to the chicken during roasting. Without it, the glaze melts off the chicken and onto the roasting pan.

You don't even always need a glaze to make these chicken legs. Simply brush them with ¼ cup Dijon mustard or barbecue sauce. Here are two ideas for how to use these simpler coatings.

Mustard-Thyme Coating

Glaze: ¼ cup Dijon mustard
Crunch: ¼ cup panko, mixed with 2 teaspoons olive oil, and ½ teaspoon dried thyme

Barbecue Coating

If your barbecue sauce is on the thin side, follow the glaze formula (page 224), replacing the preserves with the barbecue sauce.

Glaze: ¼ cup barbecue sauce
Crunch: sunflower seeds or sesame seeds

CRUNCH

This is optional, but nice! If you're in a hurry, you can omit them, but they add flavor and textural and visual interest.

- **Chopped nuts:** ¼ cup
- **Panko breadcrumbs:** ¼ cup
- **Sesame seeds:** 4 teaspoons

DOUBLE-ROASTED
CHICKEN LEGS

Serves 4

For easier cleanup, line the baking sheet with foil and coat it with vegetable cooking spray. Otherwise, the glaze that drips from the chicken during roasting will bake up as hard as lava, making the cleanup not fun!

---

4 rotisserie chicken legs (drumsticks and thighs)

1 recipe **Glaze** (see page 224)

Crunch (optional, see page 222)

---

1. Adjust the oven rack to the upper-middle position and heat the oven to 450°F. Line a small rimmed baking sheet with foil and coat with cooking spray.

2. Place the chicken legs on the baking sheet.

3. Brush the chicken legs with the **Glaze.** If desired, top with the **Crunch.** Roast the chicken legs until heated through and the glaze has set, 12 to 15 minutes. Remove from the oven, let rest a few minutes, and serve.

GLAZE FORMULA

Makes enough to glaze 4 whole chicken legs

---

2 teaspoons cornstarch

1 tablespoon **Vinegar**

¼ cup **Preserves** (see Note)

Mix the cornstarch, **Vinegar,** and 2 tablespoons water in a small cup. Add the cornstarch mixture to a small saucepan over medium-low heat, stirring constantly with a small rubber spatula until it thickens to a paste, a minute or so. Stir in the **Preserves** and remove from the heat. Proceed to step 3 on page 223.

Note: "Preserves" encompasses fruit preserves, jams, chutney, and other thick, sweet sauces, such as hoisin sauce, cranberry sauce, and marmalade.

Suggestions

For each variation, I've also suggested a crunch topping, which is both optional and interchangeable.

Cherry-Balsamic Glaze

To heighten flavor in the glaze, add ½ teaspoon minced fresh rosemary with the jam.

Vinegar: balsamic vinegar
Preserves: cherry preserves
Crunch: ¼ cup chopped pecans or almonds

Fig Glaze

Vinegar: balsamic vinegar
Preserves: fig jam
Crunch: chopped walnuts

Curry Chutney Glaze

Vinegar: rice wine vinegar
Preserves: Major Grey chutney
Crunch: ¼ cup chopped pistachios

Orange Glaze

Vinegar: sherry vinegar
Preserves: orange marmalade
Crunch: ¼ cup pepitas or chopped almonds

Hoisin Glaze

Vinegar: rice wine vinegar
Preserves: hoisin sauce
Crunch: 4 teaspoons black or white (or a combination) sesame seeds

The Broth

Since my best from-scratch chicken broth starts with a rotisserie chicken, I buy rotisserie chickens as much for the bones as for the meat. Once you've removed the legs and thighs, the breasts, and other bits of meat on the wings and the carcass, toss the remaining skin and bones, breaking the back into manageable pieces, into a large pot. Add 1 quart of chicken broth and 1½ quarts water and bring to a simmer over medium-high heat. Reduce the heat to medium-low and continue to simmer, partially covered, until the chicken pieces have given up their flavor to the broth, for about 30 minutes, and if there's time, maybe simmer a little longer. (If the broth is still simmering when the legs and thighs are done, you can toss those bones in the pot, too.) Strain, toss the bones and skin, and refrigerate or freeze the stock until ready to use.

The yield is a generous 2 quarts, or enough to make two pots of soup for 4, so consider the purchase of two rotisserie chickens a very good investment!

Unless it's a super small chicken, there should be 3 to 4 cups of extra shredded breast and other little bits of meat from the wings and back for a pot of soup, even after squirreling away the 4 cups of shredded breast meat to use in another meal.

If you choose to make another pot of soup with the second quart of broth, make it with ham or sausage. In addition to the Hearty Main Course Soup Formula on page 85, I've also included a couple of easy soup recipes (pages 226–227) that highlight the homemade broth.

SIMPLE POSOLE

Serves 4

Serve with tortilla chips and lime wedges.

---

1 tablespoon olive oil

1 medium-large onion, chopped

2 teaspoons ground cumin

1 teaspoon dried oregano

1 quart chicken broth

1 jar (16 ounces) salsa verde

3 to 4 cups shredded cooked chicken

2 cans (15 to 16 ounces each) hominy, drained

¼ cup chopped fresh cilantro

Heat the oil in a large pot over medium-high heat. Add the onion and sauté until tender, 4 to 5 minutes. Add the cumin and oregano and cook until fragrant, a minute or so longer. Add the broth, salsa, chicken, and hominy and simmer 10 minutes to blend the flavors. Stir in the cilantro. Taste and adjust the seasonings. Serve.

THAI COCONUT CHICKEN SOUP

Serves 4

Serve each portion over a cup of cooked basmati rice. If you've got fresh basil around, toss it in along with the cilantro.

---

2 tablespoons olive oil

1 large onion, chopped

1 large bell pepper, any color, stemmed, seeded and cut into medium dice

1 tablespoon minced garlic (or refrigerated paste)

1 tablespoon finely grated fresh ginger (or refrigerated paste)

2 tablespoons red curry paste

2 cups chicken broth, plus more if needed

1 can (13.5 ounces) full-fat coconut milk

3 to 4 cups shredded cooked chicken

3 tablespoons lime juice, plus lime wedges, for serving

¼ cup chopped fresh cilantro

Heat the oil in a large pot over medium-high heat. Add the onion and pepper and sauté until tender, 4 to 5 minutes. Add the garlic and ginger and cook until fragrant, a minute or so longer. Stir in the curry paste, and then add the broth, coconut milk, and chicken. Simmer 10 minutes to blend the flavors. Stir in the lime juice and cilantro. Taste and adjust the seasonings. Serve with lime wedges.

LEMON CHICKEN SOUP WITH SPINACH AND DILL

Serves 4

If you've got it, garnish the soup with crumbled feta.

---

2 tablespoons olive oil

1 onion, chopped

1½ quarts chicken broth

5 tablespoons lemon juice

3 to 4 cups shredded cooked chicken

½ cup small dried pasta, such as ditalini

2 eggs

2 egg yolks

8 ounces baby spinach

¼ cup chopped fresh dill

Salt and ground black pepper

---

1. Heat the oil in a soup kettle over medium-high heat. Add the onion and sauté until tender, 4 to 5 minutes. Add the broth, 3 tablespoons of the lemon juice, and the chicken. Bring to a simmer, reduce the heat to medium-low, and add the pasta. Continue to simmer, partially covered, until tender, 10 to 12 minutes.

2. Meanwhile, whisk the remaining 2 tablespoons lemon juice into the whole eggs and egg yolks.

3. Transfer a ladleful of the hot broth to a small bowl. Add the spinach and dill to the soup pot. Whisk the ladleful of hot broth into the eggs, then return the egg mixture to the pot and gently heat until creamy, about 1 minute longer. Remove from the heat and adjust the seasoning, including salt and pepper to taste. Serve immediately.

CHICKEN-CORN CHOWDER

Serves 4

For fresh corn, figure 3 to 4 ears for 2 cups kernels. If you've got a little parsley hanging around, chop it and add it to the pot along with the cream.

---

2 thick slices bacon, finely diced

1 large onion, chopped

3 tablespoons all-purpose flour

1 quart chicken broth

½ teaspoon dried thyme leaves

3 to 4 cups shredded cooked chicken

2 cups fresh or frozen corn kernels

½ cup heavy cream

Salt and ground black pepper

Fry the bacon in a large pot over medium-high heat until crisp, 4 to 5 minutes. Add the onion and sauté until tender, 4 to 5 minutes longer. Whisk in the flour, then the broth and thyme, and bring to a simmer. Add the chicken and corn and simmer 10 minutes to blend the flavors. Stir in the cream, heat through, and serve.

Lemon Chicken Soup
with **Spinach** *and* **Dill**

Thai Coconut
Chicken Soup

Simple Posole

The Chicken Breasts

With roasted chicken legs for dinner, a pot of stock brewing on the stove, there are two big lobes of chicken left for yet another meal *and* a pot of soup. You can cut the meat into large chunks, shred them by hand, and refrigerate. Or to quickly shred the chicken, refrigerate the chicken breasts until they are cold. Working in two batches, toss the cold chicken chunks into the bowl of a stand mixer fitted with the paddle attachment and mix until the chicken is more or less shredded, breaking up the last of the chicken chunks by hand. Do not over process.

Use the shredded breast meat to make chicken chili or one of the recipes that follow, including Quick Chicken Salad (page 235).

PULLED CHICKEN FOR
TACOS AND QUESADILLAS

Makes a generous 4 cups

Serve with crisp or soft flour or corn tortillas
and all of the trimmings you love. Some
suggestions: salsa, guacamole, sour cream or
Greek yogurt, grated sharp Cheddar, shredded
cabbage (dressed with a little olive oil, salt,
and lime juice), Pickled Pink Onions (page
53) or sliced scallions, ripe black olives,
chopped cilantro, diced tomato, your favorite
hot sauce.

2 tablespoons olive oil

1 medium-large onion, chopped

3 garlic cloves, minced

2 tablespoons chili powder

2 cups prepared salsa

4 cups shredded cooked chicken breast

½ ounce bittersweet or semisweet chocolate

Salt and ground black pepper

Heat the oil in a 12-inch skillet over medium-
high heat. Add the onion and sauté until
tender, about 4 minutes. Add the garlic and
cook until fragrant, a minute longer. Stir in
the chili powder. Stir in the salsa and chicken
and simmer over medium-low heat until the
excess liquid evaporates and flavors blend,
5 to 7 minutes. Stir in the chocolate and heat
to melt. Adjust seasonings, including salt, if
necessary, and pepper to taste. Serve.

CHICKEN CURRY

Serves 4

Sprinkle with chopped roasted peanuts or
cashews and cilantro and serve over basmati
rice or as a stew with naan bread.

2 tablespoons olive oil

1 medium-large onion, chopped

2 tablespoons curry powder

1 tablespoon grated fresh ginger (or refrigerated
ginger paste)

1 cup prepared salsa

1 can (about 13.5 ounces) coconut milk,
light or full-fat

4 cups shredded cooked chicken breast

Heat the oil in a large pot over medium-high
heat. Add the onion and sauté until tender,
about 4 minutes. Add the curry powder and
ginger and sauté until fragrant, about a
minute longer. Add the salsa, coconut milk,
and chicken and bring to a simmer. Reduce
the heat to medium-low and simmer for
10 minutes to blend the flavors. Serve.

Pulled Barbecue Chicken *for* **Tacos** *and* **Quesadillas**

PULLED BARBECUE CHICKEN

Makes about 4 cups (enough for 4 to 6 sandwiches)

Serve on toasted buns with coleslaw and/or dill pickles or make Barbecue Chicken Pizza.

2 tablespoons olive oil

1 medium-large onion, finely diced

4 cups shredded cooked chicken breast

1 cup store-bought barbecue sauce

Heat the oil in a 12-inch skillet over medium-high heat. Add the onion and sauté until tender, about 4 minutes. Add the chicken, barbecue sauce, and ¼ cup water. Reduce the heat to medium-low and simmer, stirring frequently, for 5 minutes to blend and intensify the flavors. Serve.

Note: In addition to barbecue chicken sandwiches and Barbecue Chicken Pizza, consider using Pulled Barbecue Chicken in the following simple ways:

- Serve it over a baked potato or sweet potato.

- Serve over massaged kale (page 54) that has been lightly tossed with olive oil, salt, pepper, and balsamic vinegar. Pickled Pink Onions (page 53) also make a nice addition.

BARBECUE CHICKEN PIZZA

Serves 4

2 large store-bought pizza crusts

4 cups Pulled Barbecue Chicken

2 cups grated pepper Jack cheese

1 cup or more thinly sliced red onion or Pickled Pink Onions (page 53)

Chopped fresh cilantro (optional)

Preheat the oven to 425°F. Top the crusts with the chicken, cheese, and onions. Bake until crisp and golden brown, 12 to 15 minutes. Remove from the oven and sprinkle, if you like, with chopped fresh cilantro.

QUICK CHICKEN SALAD FORMULA

Serves 6

For the herbs, extra ingredients, and dressing, see the suggestions that follow.

---

4 cups shredded cooked
chicken breast

2 medium celery stalks,
finely diced

2 medium scallions, thinly sliced

Fresh Herbs

Extra Ingredients (optional)

Dressing

Salt and ground black pepper

In a bowl, toss together the chicken, celery, scallions, **Fresh Herbs, Extra Ingredients** (if using), and **Dressing.** Taste and adjust the seasonings, including salt and pepper to taste. Serve.

— *Suggestions* —

Classic Chicken Salad

Fresh Herbs: ¼ cup chopped parsley or basil or 2 tablespoons chopped tarragon or dill
Extra Ingredients: None
Dressing: Whisk ¾ cup mayonnaise and 2 tablespoons lemon juice.

Curried Chicken Salad

Fresh Herbs: ¼ cup chopped cilantro or parsley
Extra Ingredients: 6 tablespoons dried currants or coarsely chopped raisins
Dressing: Whisk ¾ cup mayonnaise, 2 tablespoons lemon juice, 2 tablespoons Major Grey chutney, and 2 teaspoons curry powder.

Chicken Salad with Hoisin Dressing

Serve this Asian-style salad on a bed of baby spinach with sliced cucumbers and radishes. You can also roll the salad in flour tortillas with shredded watercress or arugula.

Fresh Herbs: ¼ cup chopped cilantro
Extra Ingredients: heaping ⅓ cup roasted, chopped cashews
Dressing: Whisk 6 tablespoons regular coconut milk, 2 tablespoons soy sauce, 2 tablespoons rice vinegar, 2 tablespoons hoisin sauce, 1 tablespoon finely grated fresh ginger, 1 tablespoon sesame oil, and ½ teaspoon red pepper flakes.

Thai Chicken Salad

Using the ginger paste you find in the refrigerated section of the produce department tastes like fresh and saves time.

Fresh Herbs: a generous 2 tablespoons each chopped cilantro and mint leaves
Extra Ingredients: heaping ⅓ cup chopped dry-roasted peanuts
Dressing: Whisk 6 tablespoons regular coconut milk, 2 tablespoons lime juice, 2 tablespoons fish sauce, 2 tablespoons finely grated ginger, 1 tablespoon sugar, and ½ teaspoon red pepper flakes until the sugar dissolves.

Waldorf Chicken Salad

Fresh Herbs: ¼ cup chopped parsley (optional)
Extra Ingredients: 1 large crisp apple, finely diced, heaping ⅓ cup toasted chopped walnuts
Dressing: Whisk ¾ cup mayonnaise and 2 tablespoons lemon juice.

CHICKEN
SALADS

Thai Chicken Salad

Curried Chicken Salad

Weeknight Roast Dinner

If you think roast dinners are for special occasions with
lots of prep, long roasting times, and a big cleanup,
try Weeknight Roast Dinner. You can have a small roast
seasoned and the vegetables prepped by the time the
oven preheats. After that, it's just 25 minutes of roasting.
Nothing more for you to do, so relax!

Weeknight Roast Dinner Formula

Simply coat thick-cut fish, chicken thighs, sausage, or a small pork, beef, or lamb roast with a spice rub that flavors it completely and browns it quickly, pair it with a pan full of seasonal vegetables, and pop it in a hot oven. In 25 to 30 minutes, you can be serving what might be confused with a holiday dinner—all on a Tuesday night.

PROTEIN: 1 to 2 Pounds (Depending on Cut)

When selecting fish, poultry, or meat for Weeknight Roast Dinner, choose one of three kinds of cuts: 1) cuts that stay moist and tender even when overcooked, such as chicken thighs, ham, and all kinds of sausages, 2) cuts that naturally fully cook in 25 to 30 minutes, such as pork tenderloin; and finally 3) cuts that naturally cook to medium in 20 to 30 minutes, such as thick-cut fish and beef steaks, or a rack and leg of lamb. Here are the most obvious choices:

- Center-cut salmon, left whole: 1½ pounds
- Boneless, skinless chicken thighs: 1½ to 2 pounds
- 2 small or 1 large pork tenderloin: 1¼ to 1½ pounds
- Fresh sausage links, such as Italian sausage, bratwurst, or chorizo: 1¼ to 1½ pounds
- A hunk of ham: 1 to 1½ pounds
- Cooked smoked sausages, such as kielbasa and andouille: 1 to 1½ pounds
- Large New York strip or rib-eye steaks (2 inches thick): 1¾ to 2 pounds
- Filet mignons (2½ inches thick) or 1 small beef tenderloin roast: 1¾ to 2 pounds
- 1 to 2 racks of lamb, depending on appetites: 1¼ to 2 pounds

VEGETABLES: 2½ to 3 Pounds Total (Pick 3 or 4)

The following vegetables are all ideal for the Weeknight Roast Dinner. Corn on the cob and sauerkraut aren't based on weight. With corn, figure the number of ears, and with sauerkraut, it's a cup measurement.

- **Asparagus (see Note, page 240):** Snap off tough ends.
- **Carrots or parsnips:** Peel, cut into short lengths, and halve or quarter if large.

- **Corn:** Shuck (no need to weigh—4 ears counts as 1 vegetable).
- **Beets, golden:** Peel and quarter if small; if large, cut into big chunks.
- **Bell peppers, all colors:** Quarter if small; cut into sixths if large. Seed and stem.
- **Broccoli crowns:** Halve or quarter, depending on size.
- **Brussels sprouts:** Leave whole.
- **Cabbage, small:** Halve, don't core, and cut into small wedges.
- **Cauliflower:** Trim and cut into large florets.
- **Fennel:** Trim, halve, core, and cut into quarters or sixths, depending on size.
- **Leeks:** Clip dark green leaves. Leaving root end intact, quarter lengthwise, wash thoroughly, and then cut crosswise into 3- to 4-inch lengths.
- **Mushrooms, domestic white or cremini:** Leave whole.
- **Onions, red, white, or yellow:** Leaving root end intact, peel and halve pole to pole. If small, leave as is; if medium to large, cut into thick wedges.
- **Potatoes:** No need to peel. Halve if small; if large, cut into large chunks.
- **Sauerkraut (with sausages or ham):** Drain. (No need to weigh—2 to 3 cups is one vegetable.)
- **Shallots:** Peel and leave whole.
- **Sweet potatoes:** No need to peel. Cut into 3- to 4-inch-long wedges.
- **Rutabagas:** Peel and cut into large chunks.
- **Tomatoes, cherry:** Leave whole.
- **Turnips:** Peel and quarter if small; if large, cut into big chunks.
- **Winter squash, such as butternut:** No need to peel. Seed and cut into 3- to 4-inch-long wedges.
- **Zucchini and yellow squash:** Cut crosswise into 3- to 4-inch lengths and halve (or quarter if large) into sticks.

Note: Asparagus is the only vegetable that shouldn't roast the full time. Just toss with oil, salt, and pepper and add to the roasting vegetables at the end of cooking (adding thick asparagus the last 10 to 12 minutes, medium asparagus the last 6 to 8 minutes, and thin asparagus the last 4 to 5 minutes).

MUSTARD AND THE RUB

The mustard and each ingredient in the spice rub are key to the roast's color and flavor. Ordinary salt and pepper, which enliven any cut of meat, headline the spice rub's ingredient list. Garlic powder, as well as mustard, reinforce the roast's savoriness—plus, the mustard helps the spice rub adhere.

Since these cuts roast only for 20 to 30 minutes, the brown sugar and paprika helps develop rich color. Measuring the spice rub ingredients takes only a couple of minutes. Once you measure out 2 tablespoons for today's roast dinner, there's enough for 8 more dinners to come.

RUB ADD-INS

To give your cut a distinct flavor, mix about 1 teaspoon of any of these into the 2 tablespoons of spice rub called for:

- **Dried herbs:** thyme, basil, oregano, chopped fennel seeds
- **Spices:** cumin, curry, sumac, chili powder, za'atar
- **Finely grated citrus zest:** lemon, lime, or orange
- **Fresh rosemary or thyme:** figure 2 teaspoons

ALL-PURPOSE RUB

Makes a generous 1 cup

6 tablespoons light or dark brown sugar

6 tablespoons smoked or sweet paprika (or a mixture)

3 tablespoons ground black pepper

3 tablespoons garlic powder

1½ teaspoons table salt

Mix everything together.

WEEKNIGHT ROAST DINNER

Serves 4 to 6

---

2 tablespoons **All-Purpose Rub** (page 241)

1 to 2 teaspoons **Rub Add-ins** (optional; see page 241)

1 to 2 pounds **Protein** (see page 239)

Salt and ground black pepper

1 tablespoon or so Dijon mustard

3 to 4 tablespoons olive oil

2 to 2½ pounds **Vegetables** (see pages 239 to 240)

---

1. Adjust the oven racks to the lowest and highest positions and heat the oven to 450°F. Coat one small (13 × 9-inch) and one large (18 × 12-inch) rimmed baking sheet with vegetable cooking spray.

2. Mix the **All-Purpose Rub** with the **Rub Add-ins** (if using). Lightly sprinkle the **Protein** with salt, brush all over with the mustard, coat with the spice rub, and place on the small baking sheet.

3. Working with one kind at a time, place the **Vegetables** in a medium bowl, drizzle with a tablespoon or so of oil, and sprinkle generously with salt and pepper; toss to coat. Turn them onto the large baking sheet, keeping each of the **Vegetables** separate and making sure they fit loosely in a single layer.

4. Place the vegetables on the lowest oven rack and the protein on the highest oven rack. Roast until the vegetables have cooked through, about 2½ minutes, and the protein is cooked to the desired doneness, 20 to 25 minutes. Remove from the oven and let stand for a couple of minutes. Slice or divide the cuts, if necessary, and serve.

Barbecue Chicken Dinner

Brush the chicken with barbecue sauce as it comes out of the oven and serve extra barbecue sauce mixed with the chicken juices on the side.

Protein: large boneless, skinless chicken thighs
Rub Add-in: None
Vegetables: ears of corn, cherry tomatoes, and broccoli crowns

Roast the chicken and vegetables for 25 minutes.

Pork Tenderloin with Winter Vegetables

If you like, serve the pork and vegetables with a maple-mustard dipping sauce: Just mix together ¼ cup each Dijon mustard and maple syrup.

Protein: pork tenderloin (1½ to 1¾ pounds)
Rub Add-in: 1 teaspoon dried or 2 teaspoons fresh thyme
Vegetables: Brussels spouts, onions, and butternut squash

Roast the pork tenderloin and vegetables for 25 minutes.

Classic Steak Dinner

Serve with a little sour cream mixed with horseradish or your favorite steak sauce: Figure ¼ cup sour cream and 2 tablespoons horseradish or steak sauce.

Protein: 2 rib-eye or New York strip steaks (2 inches thick) or 4 filet mignons (2½ inches thick)
Rub Add-in: none
Vegetables: mushrooms, potatoes, and broccoli crowns

Roast the steak for about 20 minutes for medium and the vegetables for 25 minutes.

Roast Salmon with Spring Vegetables

Serve with big wedges of lemon.

Protein: center-cut salmon fillet
Rub Add-in: 1 teaspoon grated lemon zest and/or minced fennel seeds or fennel pollen
Vegetables: fennel, carrots, new potatoes, and asparagus

Roast the salmon for 15 minutes and the vegetables for 25 minutes, except the asparagus (see Note, page 240).

Lamb Roast

Serve with a balsamic drizzle: Simmer ½ cup balsamic vinegar until reduced by about half. For a little extra flair, stir a little chopped fresh mint into the reduced vinegar.

Protein: 1 rack of lamb
Rub Add-in: 2 teaspoons minced fresh rosemary
Vegetables: cherry tomatoes, zucchini, potatoes, and carrots

For racks in the 1- to 1¼-pound range, roast the lamb for 20 minutes (or 25 minutes for racks over 1¼ pounds) and the vegetables for 25 minutes.

Sausages and Sauerkraut Dinner

Serve with a variety of mustards.

Protein: fresh or smoked sausages
Rub Add-in: none
Vegetables: sauerkraut, potatoes, onions, and bell peppers

Roast the sausages and vegetables for 25 minutes.

TIPS AND TRICKS

- Asparagus is the only vegetable that doesn't roast the full time (see Note, page 240).

- Broccoli and Brussels sprouts fully cook with 20 to 25 minutes roasting time. If you prefer them less cooked, toss them in after 10 minutes.

- As long as you're not overcrowding the pans, you can increase either protein or vegetables to serve dinner for 6 and in some cases, up to 8 (or leftovers for 4)!

WEEKNIGHT ROAST DINNER

1. Adjust oven racks to the lowest and highest positions and heat the oven to 450°F.

2. Lightly sprinkle the protein with salt, brush with the mustard, coat with the spice rub, and place on a small rimmed baking sheet.

3. Toss each vegetable with olive oil, salt, and pepper and arrange on a large rimmed baking sheet.

4. Place the protein on the top oven rack and the vegetables on the lowest rack and roast vegetables 25 minutes and protein 15 to 25 minutes, depending on cut.

Shove-It-in-the-Oven Stew

Cassoulet-Style Italian Sausages was one of the most
popular recipes in my sixth book—*Perfect One-Dish
Dinners.* Everyone loved it because prep time was
so low and the taste factor so high. How many satisfying
dishes are as simple as tossing a few sausages
into a roasting pan (along with onion, garlic, cherry
tomatoes, thyme, and an oil and vinegar drizzle), shoving it
in the oven for 45 minutes, stirring in a few cans
of beans, and then popping it back in the oven to heat
through? The result: a dish simple enough for weeknight
supper, yet impressive enough for a nice dinner.

Shove-It-in-the-Oven Stew Formula

After the success of the Cassoulet-Style Italian Sausages recipe in my previous book, I wanted more of these quick, simple stews in my repertoire that didn't require all the usual time-consuming steps like browning meat and sautéing vegetables, so I tried a chicken version, subbing boneless, skinless chicken thighs for the sausage, spring vegetables for the tomatoes, and potatoes for the white beans. I'll be darned if this dish wasn't just as amazingly simple and wonderfully tasty as the sausage dish, so I tried another. By adding shrimp at the 45-minute mark a la the white beans, I realized fish and shellfish could work as well, so I developed a Mediterranean seafood stew with fennel and orange and a little red pepper flakes. That dish was a big hit, too.

I was onto something. No stranger to seeing the pattern in seemingly different recipes, I realized these shove-it dishes could be reduced to a formula. The roasting pan's wide surface, the oven's high heat, and arranging the ingredients in a more or less single layer mean the meat, onions, garlic, and vegetables have an opportunity to "sauté" before they start to release their juices. Here's how the formula works.

ONION

Every good stew needs onions, and all of the shove-it stews start with them. As for the onion type, I suggest a particular one for each stew, but they are totally interchangeable. If the stew you want to make calls for a sweet white and you only have a red onion in your vegetable basket, use it.

Of course, the leek's green hues beautify a stew, and its mild yet complex taste is unique. Still, if you don't have time to prepare (or can't find) leeks, use a sweet white onion instead. And when you're really pressed for time, snip open a bag of frozen pearl onions.

- 1 large red, yellow, or sweet white onion: Peel and cut into large dice.

- A nice bunch of leeks (2 to 3): Trim off the tough dark green tops and discard. Quarter lengthwise, then cut crosswise into ½-inch-thick slices. Wash in a bowl of cold water.

- 1 bag (1 pound) frozen pearl onions: Snip open the bag and dump into the roasting pan.

Shove-It-in-the-Oven Chicken Tangine

PROTEIN (POULTRY, PORK, OR SEAFOOD): 2 to 2½ Pounds

The protein needs to be relatively quick-cooking, so classic stewing meats like beef, pork, and lamb are out; but poultry, ham, smoked pork chops, and sausages of all varieties work. And with their shorter cooking times, seafood and shellfish can be added at the 45-minute mark with other last-minute ingredients. Here are some of your best protein choices:

- **Sausages, fresh links (pork or poultry):** Cut into about 3-inch lengths.
- **Sausages, cured or smoked links (pork or poultry):** Cut into about 3-inch lengths.
- **Chunk of ham:** Cut or shred into large chunks.
- **Boneless, skinless chicken thighs:** Cut into large chunks.
- **Firm-fleshed fish (such as cod or salmon):** Cut into large chunks.
- **Large shrimp:** Peeled and devein.

VEGETABLES: 1½ to 2 Pounds

Carrots and other root vegetables like winter squash, turnips, and rutabagas all make great stew vegetables, as do cabbage, cauliflower, and mushrooms. Cherry tomatoes are perfect for shove-it stews because they don't release their juices until the end of cooking, which means the protein, onions, garlic, and other vegetables have a chance to sauté before stewing.

- **Apples, firm, crisp (such as Granny Smith):** Though not a vegetable, apples work well with sausages and chicken thighs. Halve, core, and cut into 6 wedges.
- **Bell peppers:** Halve, stem, seed, and cut into 6 wedges.
- **Cabbage, small:** Halve and cut into 6 to 8 wedges.
- **Carrots:** Peel, halve, seed, and cut into large chunks.
- **Cauliflower:** Core and cut into large florets or buy packaged cauliflower florets.
- **Celery:** Cut into large chunks.
- **Fennel:** Trim fronds and stalks; reserve fronds. Halve bulb and cut into 6 to 8 wedges, depending on size.
- **Mushrooms, domestic white or baby bella:** Leave whole if small; halve if medium; quarter if large.
- **Tomatoes, cherry or grape:** Leave whole.
- **Turnips or rutabagas:** Peel, halve, seed, and cut into large chunks.
- **Yellow squash or zucchini:** Trim ends and cut into large chunks.
- **Winter squash:** Peel, halve, seed, and cut into large chunks.

STARCH

You can use all one kind of starch or half and half, e.g., black beans and hominy or potatoes and corn. When using a mix of canned beans and frozen corn, figure 2 cans beans and 1 package (12 ounces) frozen corn.

- 1 pound potatoes (including sweet potatoes), halved if small or cut into large dice
- 3 cans (15 to 16 ounces each) beans (white, black, kidney, pinto or chickpeas). Drain black beans only. The rest you can add to the roasting pan straight from the can. Add beans during the last 10 to 15 minutes of cooking.
- 3 cans (15 to 16 ounces each) hominy, drained. Add for the last 10 to 15 minutes of cooking.
- 1 bag (16 ounces) frozen corn, thawed. Add for the last 10 to 15 minutes of cooking.
- 4 cups cooked grains, lentils, pasta, or rice. If you've cooked grains or pasta (see "A Little Mise," page 34), you can add them to Shove-It-in-the-Oven dishes as well. Stir them in the last 10 to 15 minutes as you would canned beans.

ACID

All the Shove-It-in-the-Oven dishes benefit from acidity. Adding vinegar is easy—just dump 2 to 3 tablespoons in up front with the rest of the ingredients. You can also use ½ cup reduced wine. Take time to reduce it while the stew is in the oven, and stir it in at the end of cooking along with the finishers. The reduced wine will make the stew taste like it's been simmering for hours.

To reduce wine quickly: Bring 2 cups wine to a boil in a large skillet over high heat. Continue to boil until reduced to ½ cup, 8 to 10 minutes.

ADDITIONAL FLAVORINGS (Optional, but Often Nice)

- ¾ cup dried fruits, such as prunes, apricots, and cranberries
- 1 cup whole olives, any kind, pitted unless you warn diners that they're not!
- ¾ cup chopped sun-dried tomatoes
- ½ cup drained capers

DRIED HERBS/SPICES/ZESTS

As with most of the other formulas in this book, add dried herbs, spices, and zests at the beginning of cooking so that they have time to infuse the dish with flavor. In this formula, fresh herbs are considered Finishers and offer a burst of flavor at the end of cooking.

FINISHERS

Whether it's broth to moisten, cream to enrich, cornstarch to thicken, chopped fresh herbs to enliven, or reduced wine to add depth, most of these stews require a little finishing at the end. Use your judgment. Look at the stew, taste the stew, and decide. If it's not juicy enough, add broth. If it's too juicy, stir in a little cornstarch mixed with water. If it tastes wan, remember that a sprinkling of salt or a little drizzle of acid (e.g., vinegar, lemon juice, or reduced wine) will go a long way toward improving flavor. Fresh herbs add great flavor as well.

TIPS AND TRICKS

- If you're looking for shortcuts, don't use jarred minced garlic. Instead, pick up a small Cryovac package or plastic tub of peeled garlic, which you'll find in the produce department. Its shelf life is quite long, but buy it in quantities you can go through before it softens.

- Once you get comfortable with the formula, start to play. Use 1 to 1½ pounds sausage and 2 pounds of shellfish like mussels or clams for a satisfying sausage and seafood stew. Add shellfish at the end of cooking, cover the pan with foil, return it to the oven and cook until the shells open.

- Leftover stew is easily transformed into soup on another night with the addition of chicken broth to thin it out.

SHOVE-IT-IN-THE-OVEN STEW

Serves 6 to 8

Onion: 1 large onion or 1 bag (1 pound) frozen pearl onions

6 to 8 garlic cloves, sliced

1½ to 2 pounds **Vegetables** (see page 253)

2 to 2½ pounds **Protein** (see page 253)

Starch (see page 254)

¼ cup olive oil (see Note)

Acid: 2 to 3 tablespoons vinegar or ½ cup reduced wine (see page 254)

Additional Flavorings (optional; see page 254)

Salt and ground black pepper

Dried Herbs/Spices/Zests (see page 255)

Finishers: fresh herbs, broth (chicken or fish depending on protein), ½ cup heavy cream, or 1 tablespoon cornstarch dissolved in 3 tablespoons cold water

1. Adjust the oven rack to the lowest position and heat the oven to 450°F.

2. Scatter the **Onion**, garlic, **Vegetables, Protein** (if using pork or chicken), and **Starch** (if using potatoes) in a large roasting pan. Drizzle with the olive oil and **Acid** (if using vinegar). Sprinkle generously with salt and pepper, along with the **Dried Herbs/Spices/Zests** and toss to combine.

3. Place in the oven, uncovered, and stew until all of the ingredients are fully cooked, about 45 minutes. At this point, you can remove the pan from the oven unless you are using seafood as your **Protein,** or are including beans, hominy, corn, or cooked grains as your **Starch.** Add those to the pan, return to the oven, and roast until the seafood is just cooked and the dish is warmed through, 8 to 10 minutes longer.

4. Set the pan over 2 burners over medium heat. Stir in the **Finishers.** If using the reduced wine as your **Acid,** add it now as well. Taste and adjust the seasonings, including salt and pepper. Serve.

Note: You may find some of your stew combinations could benefit from a little bacon or prosciutto: Figure 4 ounces bacon, cut into small dice, or 2 ounces prosciutto, minced. If using either of them, reduce the oil to 3 tablespoons and add the bacon or prosciutto to the pan at the beginning, along with the protein and vegetables.

Ratatouille Stew

This stew is especially perfect when end-of-summer vegetables are so abundant.

Onion: red onion
Vegetables: 1 small eggplant, 1 small yellow bell pepper, 1 small zucchini, and 1 pint cherry tomatoes
Protein: Italian sausage, chicken thighs, or fish
Starch: white beans
Acid: balsamic vinegar
Additional Flavorings: none
Dried Herbs/Spices/Zests: 2 teaspoons herbes de Provence
Finishers: ¼ cup each chopped fresh parsley and basil

Follow the Shove-It-in-the-Oven Stew technique and stir in the white beans (and fish, if using) after 45 minutes.

Roast Italian Sausages with Potatoes and Cabbage

This easy one-dish dinner is perfect when the weather starts to chill.

Onion: sweet onion
Vegetables: 1 pound each cabbage and carrots
Protein: sweet or hot Italian sausage or kielbasa
Starch: new, fingerling, or boiling potatoes
Acid: apple cider vinegar
Additional Flavorings: none
Dried Herbs/Spices/Zests: 2 teaspoons caraway seeds and a couple of bay leaves
Finishers: chicken broth

Shove-It-in-the-Oven Chicken Tagine with Apricots and Almonds

Sprinkle this dish with almonds, preferably Marcona, which are pretty widely available. If you can't find them, simply fry ½ cup slivered almonds in ¼ cup oil in a small skillet over medium heat, stirring occasionally, until golden brown, about 2 minutes; remove with a slotted spoon. Or, just sprinkle the dish with chopped roasted almonds.

Onion: yellow or sweet onion
Vegetables: 4 large carrots and 3 medium zucchini
Protein: boneless, skinless chicken thighs
Starch: canned chickpeas
Acid: red wine vinegar
Additional Flavorings: coarsely chopped apricots
Dried Herbs/Spices/Zests: Mix together 2 teaspoons ground cinnamon, 2 teaspoons ground ginger, 1 teaspoon turmeric, and 1 teaspoon ground black pepper
Finishers: ½ cup chopped fresh cilantro and broth as needed

Mediterranean Shrimp Stew

This easy one-dish stew uses the fennel bulb as one of the stew's vegetables and its fronds for finishing. Don't leave out the grated orange zest—it's key to this stew's flavor. If you like, add the juice of the orange to the stew along with the zest.

Onion: yellow or sweet onion
Vegetables: 2 pints cherry tomatoes and 2 medium fennel bulbs (save the fronds)
Protein: large peeled shrimp
Starch: new, fingerling, or boiling potatoes
Acid: reduced white wine
Additional Flavorings: none
Dried Herbs/Spices/Zests: 1½ teaspoons fennel seeds, 1½ teaspoons finely grated orange zest
Finishers: fish broth, if necessary, and ½ cup chopped fennel fronds

Shove-It-in-the-Oven Chicken Tagine

Shove-It-in-the-Oven Creamy Spring Chicken Stew

Offering all the comfort of winter and all the vibrancy and beauty of spring, this stew is perfect for a cool spring night.

Onion: Leeks
Vegetables: 1 pound each carrots and mushrooms
Protein: boneless, skinless chicken thighs
Starch: small potatoes (red, yellow, purple, or a mix of all 3), halved
Acid: reduced white wine
Additional Flavorings: none
Dried Herbs/Spices/Zests: 2 teaspoons dried tarragon
Finishers: heavy cream and chicken broth if needed

Shove-It-in-the-Oven Chicken (or Sausage) Stew with Apples and Cabbage

Onion: yellow or sweet onion
Vegetables: 1 pound or so each crisp apples and cabbage wedges
Protein: boneless, skinless chicken thighs or sausages of any kind, including kielbasa
Starch: new or boiling potatoes
Acid: balsamic vinegar or reduced white wine
Additional Flavorings: none
Dried Herbs/Spices/Zests: 2 teaspoons dried thyme leaves
Finishers: chicken broth

Follow the Shove-It-in-the-Oven Stew technique. If using vinegar, add it before the dish goes in the oven. If using reduced wine, add it with the finishers.

Shove-It-in-the Oven Chili Chicken (or Chorizo) Stew with Black Beans and Corn

Onion: yellow or sweet onion
Vegetables: 2 pints cherry tomatoes and 1 large bell pepper
Protein: boneless, skinless chicken thighs or chorizo (or a mix)
Starch: 2 cans black beans and 1 bag frozen corn
Acid: Red wine vinegar or sherry vinegar
Additional Flavorings: none
Dried Herbs/Spices/Zests: 2 tablespoons chili powder and 2 teaspoons dried oregano
Finishers: ½ cup chopped fresh cilantro

Coq au Vin, Shove-It-in-the-Oven Style

Bacon contributes to the Coq au Vin's rich flavor here.

Onion: frozen pearl onions
Vegetables: mushrooms and carrots
Protein: boneless, skinless chicken thighs
Starch: potatoes
Acid: reduced red wine
Additional Flavorings: bacon (see Note, page 257)
Dried Herbs/Spices/Zests: 1½ teaspoons dried thyme leaves
Finishers: chicken broth and 1 tablespoon cornstarch mixed with 3 tablespoons water

Pozole con Pollo

Onion: sweet onion
Vegetables: 1½ pounds (about 3 pints) cherry tomatoes and 1 bell pepper
Protein: 1½ pounds boneless, skinless chicken thighs and 1 pound chorizo sausage
Starch: hominy
Acid: sherry vinegar
Additional Flavorings: 1 cup small pimiento-stuffed olives
Dried Herbs/Spices/Zests: 2 tablespoons smoked paprika, 1 tablespoon dried oregano, ½ teaspoon red pepper flakes
Finishers: ½ cup chopped fresh cilantro

At a Glance

SHOVE-IT-IN-THE-OVEN STEW

1. Toss all the ingredients (know the exceptions) in a heavy-duty roasting pan.

2. Roast in a 450°F oven until fully cooked and stew-like, about 45 minutes. If using one of the exception ingredients, add it now and return the stew to the oven.

3. Set the roasting pan over 2 burners over medium heat and stir in the finishers. Adjust the seasonings.

Thanks to

———

My French friend and surrogate mother, Betty Beccari, who taught me that eating well can be simple, fresh, and classy.

My daughter and son-inlaw, Sharon and Anthony Damelio, whose cooking style always inspires me and is evident throughout this book, especially in "A Little Mise."

My agent and friend, Sarah Jane Freymann, who for the last two decades has thoughtfully and lovingly shepherded my books to publication.

My editor, Jennifer Sit, as well as senior art director Stephanie Huntwork and senior designer Mia Johnson, whose smart vision transformed a quirky two-decades-old cookbook into one that is clean, clear, and classy.

Production editor Joyce Wong, production manager Kim Tyner, and copy editor Kate Slate, who helped get the book right and keep it on track.

Photographer Lauren Volo and stylist Mariana Velasquez, who miraculously transformed utilitarian formulas and techniques into pages of beauty.

Index